retail and restaurant spaces

An International Portfolio of 41 Designers

GLOUCESTER MASSACHUSETTS

ROCKPORT PUBLISHERS

kristen richards

First published in the United States of America by
Rockport Publishers, Inc.
33 Commercial Street
Gloucester, Massachusetts 01930-5089
Telephone: (978) 282-9590
Facsimile: (978) 283-2742

Distributed to the book trade and art trade
in the United States by
North Light Books, an imprint of
F & W Publications
1507 Dana Avenue
Cincinnati, Ohio 45207
Telephone: (800) 289-0963

Other distribution by
Rockport Publishers, Inc.
Gloucester, Massachusetts 01930-5089

ISBN 1-56496-488-4

10 9 8 7 6 5 4 3 2 1

Design: SYP Design & Production
www.sypdesign.com

Frontispiece: Elkus/Manfredi Architects Ltd.
  Artful Hand Gallery, Photo: Marco Lorenzetti/
  Hedrich Blessing

FRONT COVER IMAGE
Photo: Sharon Risedorph
Design Firm: John Lum Architecture
Location: Paradis, Palo Alto, California

BACK COVER IMAGES
LEFT
Photo: Gerald Lopez
Design Firm: Axis Network
Location: The Straits Restaurant, Radisson Plaza,
Kuala Lumpur, Malaysia

MIDDLE
Photo: John Drooyan
Design Firm: AkarStudio
Location: Mi Piace, Los Angeles, California

RIGHT
Photo: Todd Eberle
Design Firm: David Ling Architecture
Location: Philosophy Boutique for Alberta Ferretti,
New York, New York

Printed in China.

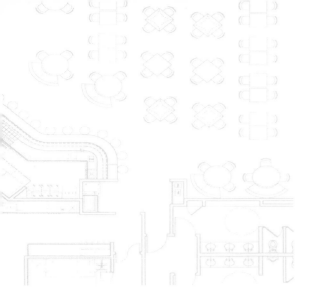

CONTENTS

Foreword   6
by David Rockwell

Introduction   7
by Kristen Richards

AkarStudio   8
Mi Piace, Los Angeles, California
American Bistro, Thousand Oaks, California

Architectural Alliance   12
Caribou Coffee, Brooklyn Park, Minnesota
Caribou Coffee, Woodbury, Minnesota
Sola Squeeze, Minneapolis, Minnesota

Aria Group Architects, Inc.   16
Brio, Blue Chip Casino,
    Michigan City, Indiana
Ventura Lounge, Blue Chip, Casino,
    Michigan City, Indiana
Heaven on Seven, Chicago, Illinois
56 West, Chicago, Illinois

Axis Network   20
Cilantro, Micasa Hotel, Kuala Lumpur, Malaysia
Trilogy Café, Bangsar, Kuala Lumpur, Malaysia
Straits Restaurant, Radisson Plaza,
    Kuala Lumpur, Malaysia
Haute Coiffure Salon,
    Starhill Shopping Centre,
    Kuala Lumpur, Malaysia

Bergmeyer Associates   24
Boston Museum of Fine Arts Museum
    Store, Boston, Massachusetts
Commonwealth Brewing Company,
    Rockefeller Center, New York, New York
Dick's Clothing and Sporting Goods,
    Columbia, Maryland
Levi Strauss Dockers Store, Troy, Michigan
AKRIS, Boston, Massachusetts

LIEBER COOPER ASSOCIATES   CAFE SPIAGGIA   PHOTO: MARK BALLOGG, STEINKAMP/BALLOGG

Bogdanow Partners   30
Union Pacific Restaurant, New York, New York
Merchants, New York, New York, New York
Rain, New York, New York

Brennan Beer Groman Monk   34
Transporter: Movies You Ride,
    Empire State Building,
    New York, New York
Comp USA, Fifth Avenue, New York, New York
Peninsula Hong Kong Hotel Restaurant, Hong Kong

Clodagh Design International   38
Nöelle Spa for Beauty & Wellness,
    Stamford, Connecticut
Felissimo, New York, New York

CREAR-Jamie Bouzaglo   42
Diva Discotheque, Montréal, Canada
Bice Ristorante, Montréal, Canada
Coppola Boutique, Montréal, Canada
Mediterraneo, Montréal, Canada
Prímadonna Restaurant, Montréal, Canada

Cuningham Group   46
Star Trek: The Experience, Las Vegas, Nevada
Rainforest Café, Disney Marketplace,
     Lake Buena Vista, Florida
Café Odyssey, Mall of America, Bloomington, Minnesota

Desgrippes Gobé and Associates   50
Ann Taylor, Madison Avenue, New York, New York
Liz Claiborne, New York, New York
Rockport Company, New York, New York

Elkus/Manfredi Architects, Ltd.   54
The Artful Hand, Boston, Massachusetts
PapaRazzi's Cucina Restaurant,
     Peabody, Massachusetts
World of Disney Store, Downtown Disney,
     Orlando, Florida
Foot Locker, Watertown, Massachusetts
Kids Foot Locker, Watertown, Massachusetts

Engstrom Design Group   60
California Café, Denver, Colorado
California Café Bar and Grill, Chicago, Illinois
Nordstrom Café, Atlanta, Georgia
Vertigo, TransAmerica Tower, San Francisco, California

FRCH Design Worldwide   66
Harrah's, Las Vegas, Nevada
Tempus Expeditions, Mall of America,
     Bloomington, Minnesota
OshKosh B'Gosh, Leawood, Kansas
Eddie Bauer, San Francisco, California
Eddie Bauer, Michigan Avenue, Chicago, Illinois

Franke, Gottsegen, Cox Architects   72
Barney Greengrass, Barney's New York,
     Beverly Hills, California
O'Padeiro, New York, New York
Aveda, New York, New York

Gensler   76
Universal Studios Store, Hollywood, California
The North Face, Flagship Shop, Chicago, Illinois
Compaq Works, Houston, Texas
Slick Willie's Bayou Place, Houston, Texas
HomeChef, Palo Alto, California
San Francisco Museum of Modern Art
     Museum Store, San Francisco, California
SOMA Living, San Francisco, California

GRID/3 International   82
Audi Park Avenue, New York, New York
Christian Bernard, Roosevelt Field Mall,
     Long Island, New York
Color Siete, Bogotá, Columbia

Haverson Architecture and Design P.C.   86
Spiga Ristorante, New York, New York
Motown Café, New York Hotel and Casino,
     Las Vegas, Nevada
Turnbull & Asser, New York, New York
Harley-Davidson Café, Las Vegas, Nevada

Hirsch Bedner Associates   90
Café Blue Veranda, Hotel Inter-Continental,
     Tokyo Bay, Toyko
Hyatt Regency Aruba, Dining Room, Aruba
     Café Carnaval, Westin Rio Mar Resort,
     Puerto Rico
Portofino Restaurant, Sheraton Desert Inn,
     Las Vegas, Nevada
La Cucina, Hotel Europa & Regina, Venice, Italy
Ho Wan, Sheraton Desert Inn, Las Vegas, Nevada

IIDA Singapore Pte, Ltd.   94
Kublai Khan Restaurant, Park Mall Shopping
     Centre, Singapore
Ninth Street Pub/Disco, Taiwan
Coral and Shell Club, Boat Quay, Singapore
Ninth Street Pub, Taiwan

The International Design Group, Inc.   98
Runners'Choice, Toronto, Canada
Famous Players Silver City, Toronto, Canada
Bailey, Banks & Biddle, Philadelphia, Pennsylvania
Bottle Your Own, Toronto, Canada
La Maison Simons Department Store, Québec, Canada

JGA, Inc.   102
Warner Bros., Fifth Avenue, New York, New York
Camelot Music, Great Lakes Mall, Ohio
Brookstone, New York, New York
Café Site, Seoul, Korea
Giorgio Beverly Hills, Beverly Hills, California
Elizabeth Arden Red Door Salon and Spa,
     Madison Avenue, New York, New York
Fossil, Columbus, Ohio

Planungsgruppe Jöhnk   108
Nordsee, Frankfurt, Germany
Bistro Blechnapf, Neumünster, Germany
FEC II Brewery, Stuttgart, Germany
Stuttgart Candy Shop, Stuttgart, Germany
Rockcafe, FEC II Brewery, Stuttgart, Germany

SFJones-Architects   112
La Maison du Cigar, Beverly Hills, California
David Paul's Diamond Head Grill, Colony
     Surf Hotel, Honolulu, Hawaii
The Hump, Santa Monica Airport,
     Santa Monica, California

LeMay Michaud Architecture Design   116
Bistango, Québec, Canada
Pointe des Amérique, Montréal, Canada
Bar Biloxi, Montréal, Canada
Café de Monde, Québec, Canada

Lieber Cooper Associates   120
Big Downtown, Palmer House, Chicago, Illinois
Café Spiaggia, Chicago, Illinois
Palmer House Hilton, Main Dining Room, Chicago, Illinois
Stir Crazy, Northbrook, Illinois
Fulton's Crab House, Pleasure Island,
    Walt Disney World Resort,
    Orlando, Florida

David Ling Architects   124
Philosophy Boutique for Alberta Ferretti,
    New York, New York
Apollo Bar, Cologne, Germany

John Lum Architecture   128
Paradis, Palo Alto, California
Asia SF, San Francisco, California
Dr. Jimmy Fong Optometry, San Francisco, California
Urban Eyes Optometry, San Francisco, California

Michael Malone Architects, Inc.   132
Voyagers: The Travel Store, Plano, Texas
Shell Oils' Encompass Store, Houston, Texas
Blue Canoe, Seattle, Washington
Discovery Channel Store, The Galleria, Houston, Texas

Patrick McBride Company   136
Coco Marina, New York, New York
Tuscan Square, Rockfeller Center,
    New York, New York
The Hard Rock Café, Key West, Florida
Jimmy Buffet's Margaritaville Store,
    Charleston, South Carolina

Jordan Mozer & Associates   140
Surf'n Turf, Matsuyama, Japan
Cypress Club, Chicago, Illinois
Cheesecake Factory, Chicago, Illinois

NBBJ   144
Mr. Rags, Bellevue, Washington
Puget Consumers Co-op, Seattle, Washington

Rockwell Group   148
Next Door Nobu, New York, New York
Best Cellars, New York, New York
Payard Patisserie and Bistro, New York, New York
Monkey Bar, New York, New York
Baang, Aspen, Colorado
Nobu, New York, New York

Rita St. Clair Associates   154
Charleston Restaurant, Baltimore, Maryland
Polo Grill, Baltimore, Maryland
Peabody Court Restaurant/Conservatory,
    Baltimore, Maryland

Shea Architects, Inc.   158
The Cup, University of Minnesota
Goodfellow's, Minneapolis, Minnesota
Tejas, Edina, Minnesota
Famous Dave's, Forest Lake, Minnesotaa

Earl Swensson Associates, Inc.   162
Beauregard's, Opryland Hotel and Convention Center,
    Nashville, Tennessee
Wildhorse Saloon, Nashville, Tennessee

Mathias Thörner Design, Inc.   166
Timberland, Chicago, Illinois
Britches, Georgetown, Washington, D.C.

II By IV Design Associates   170
Oro, Toronto, Canada
Moishes, Toronto, Canada
Marccain, Toronto, Canada
Zoom, Toronto, Canada

Jean-Pierre Viau Design   174
Platine, Montréal, Canada
Orbite Coupe Beauté, Montréal, Canada
Thaï Grill, Montréal, Canada
Mikado, Montréal, Canada
Pizzédélic, Montréal, Canada

Yabu Pushelberg   178
ClearNet, Toronto, Canada
Holt Renfrew, Toronto, Canada
Monsoon, Toronto, Canada

Robert Young Associates   184
I.N.C., Macy's Herald Square, New York
Beretta Gallery, Dallas, Texas
Neiman Marcus, Beverly Hills, California
Neiman Marcus-North Park, Dallas, Texas

Directory of Firms   188

Directory of Establishments   190

FOREWORD

This volume immerses the reader in a series of exceptional retail and restaurant projects. The trained eye will pore over these selections and pinpoint the conceptual approach taken by each designer. At the same time, it will search out answers to the basic design questions we always ask ourselves:

Who is the client and what are its goals?

Who are the customers, visitors, or guests and what are they looking for?

Where is the location geographically, socially, and historically?

How does the menu or product relate to the project design?

What kind of message do we want to communicate?

Answers to these questions will provide a plethora of details. Undoubtedly, pragmatists will find many of them helpful and consider them a source book on inventive and practical solutions to the problems we confront in our own work.

From my point of view, these efforts offer a more esoteric opportunity. Looking at this work prompts me to investigate and reflect upon the act of creating dynamic commercial spaces. I am most interested in spaces that achieve the goal of becoming individual communities. Each community brings people together. Each spices our lives with moments of pure pleasure.

Trace that pleasure to its origins and you will discover two factors: the practical and aesthetic concerns of the owner

and the eye of the designer. Tempering imagination with pragmatic constraint, the designer focuses the concerns of the owner. At best, the collaboration produces a destination that deserves to be called "special."

To me, the best of these destinations are equivalent to stage sets. These theaters of everyday life allow people to engage in private interactions in a public place. The formal and the casual inevitably overlap. The planned and the unpredictable merge, producing a public celebration.

The creation of a designed space is an exercise in total control. To succeed, the planning and construction must be executed with the utmost precision. So, let us, in the end, celebrate the one thing that can not be controlled: the behavior and emotional lives of those who choose to enter these spaces.

Whenever a designer utilizes his or her wit and style to create spaces that facilitate that behavior, individuals stand a chance of having a pleasurable experience. The more pleasurable the experience, the greater the likelihood the customer will pay repeated visits.

Take another look at these stores and restaurants. Evaluate the theatrical quality of each. Decide which encourage and enhance spontaneity and a sense of joy. This winning combination usually produces a space that you will remember as special.

David Rockwell
Founder, Rockwell Group

ROCKWELL GROUP   NEXT DOOR NOBU   PHOTO: PAUL WARCHOL

INTRODUCTION

Stores and restaurants are facing challenges that go well beyond dealing with competitors. Catalogues, Web sites, and e-commerce are making the world smaller and consumers more sophisticated. (It is estimated that on-line shopping will reach $1 trillion by 2005). Built environments must be compelling; combining product, value, and experience to keep customers coming through their doors to spend their time— and money. And with a growing global economy and culture, retail and restaurant interiors require distinctive yet universally understood identities.

The projects showcased in this book are meant to be more than just "eye candy" for the coffee table. They represent benchmarks for innovative, imaginative, and, in many cases, daring design. The intent in compiling this showcase of *Retail and Restaurants* is to present as broad a range of projects as possible—from the serene to the interactive, the traditional to the exotic; from multinational retailers to unique specialty boutiques, and from five-star gourmet restaurants to funky coffee bars.

There is a bit of irony in the book: I have a near-phobia when it comes to shopping that goes back to my teens, and I seldom eat out. But my greatest professional satisfaction over the past ten years has come from writing about remarkable retail and restaurant environments. And, luckily, I have no fear of asking questions at a construction site: What is it going to be? Who owns it? And who's designing it? That approach has allowed me to meet—and often befriend—the many gifted designers, their clients, and the photographers who make these pages so beautiful.

Kristen Richards

FRCH DESIGN WORLDWIDE   TEMPUS EXPEDITIONS   PHOTO: DAN FORER

AKARSTUDIO

Sanskrit for "form," *akar* is the force behind AkarStudio's atypical approach to projects. Seeking out uncharted courses in retail and hospitality design, AkarStudio strives to explore whimsical aspects of form and shape, combining them into inventive and contemporary architectural design solutions. The firm uses the interplay of layers and textures, combined with strong color palettes and the relationship between fluid shapes and geometric lines, to create a singular style. The diversity of the designers, resourceful concepts, and strong technical expertise take clients smoothly from design development to final construction.

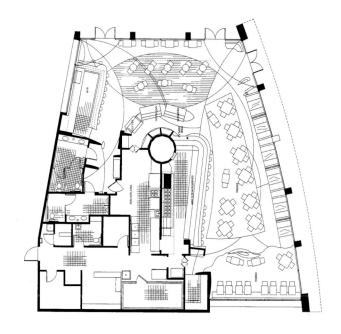

(top) The casual nature of the café and bakery area of Mi Piace in Los Angeles is expressed by simple wood pedestal tables and brightly colored seating. (floor plan, right)

(opposite) Sculptural ceiling elements animate Mi Piace—and define different areas. A colorful, Calder-like glass and metal mobile highlights the café section, and a mythical boat form floats over the dining room.

ALL PHOTOS: JOHN DROOYAN

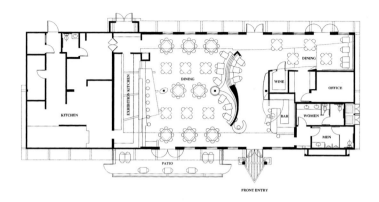

(above) A suspended circular ceiling canopy, pendant fixtures, and stone-topped bar create a congenial, intimate space within American Bistro in Thousand Oaks, California. (floor plan, above)

(right) American Bistro's open exhibition kitchen sparkles with copper accents overhead. A two-level, stone-topped counter borders the kitchen and is ideal for grabbing a quick bite.

ARCHITECTURAL ALLIANCE INC.

Architectural Alliance takes pride in its personalized and highly professional service, developing long standing client relationships that have extended over twenty years. Based on mutual trust and respect, this relationship has produced award-winning designs that are creative, functional, and responsive to their physical and cultural context. As its name implies, the firm has become successful through team building as an approach to design, and encourages strong partnering relationships between employees, clients, contractors, and consultants. It has a strong base of work for a wide range of clients including corporations, governments, institutions, property managers, retailers, airlines, and airports in both renovation and new construction.

(top) Since 1992, Caribou Coffee has grown to more than 113 stores. Its rapid, national expansion required a unique brand identity in the ever-growing gourmet coffee bar market, resulting in the Caribou Lodge concept.

(right) Caribou Coffee in Brooklyn Park, Minnesota, embodies the full lodge concept with a fireplace that anchors several different areas.

(opposite) Every Caribou Coffee now uses pine and stone to establish a modern interpretation of a rustic yet comfortable lifestyle.
ALL PHOTOS: DON WONG

(right) The Woodbury, Minnesota, store is the first Caribou Coffee to incorporate a "lodge" aesthetic within the sleek lines and modern materials that Caribou had been using.

(below, top) Sola Squeeze is a new juice bar concept offering smoothie drinks that blend fruits, vegetables, and nutritional supplements. Sola Squeeze is designed to be upscale, hip, and elegant—with a "natural" slant.

(below, bottom) The Sola Squeeze tagline, "A Blend of Sun and Earth," is exuberantly translated in the design. Sun and earth are symbolically represented in forms, colors, and textures to call to mind the natural land/sky connections to the natural ingredients used in the drinks. A total brand identity for Sola Squeeze was developed in cooperation with Kilter, Inc.

ARIA GROUP ARCHITECTS, INC.

Sensitive to the importance of staying within an established budget, Aria Group Architects, Inc., (AGA) is known for creating an imaginative and well-balanced design that relates to the end-user. AGA perceives the construction of a project as a team effort with the owner, architect, and contractor working together towards a common goal. Founded in 1989 by James Lencioni, Walter Pancewicz, Joseph Vajda, and Kathy Lencioni, the firm's goal is to provide personalized architectural and interior design services to clients, combining a high standard of design with fiscal responsibility. AGA continually strives for a highly creative, personalized design solution that not only fulfills the clients' needs, but also responds to the realistic constraints of budget, schedule, and technology.

(right) Created to provide a complete departure from the Art Deco style of most of Blue Chip Casino's docking pavilion, in Michigan City, Indiana, Brio is a colorful restaurant designed to capture the feeling of a coastal Italian eatery.

(opposite, top) The Ventura Lounge at the Blue Chip is a colorful venue designed with an urban Deco slant, using dark woods and classic colors. Raised booths, cocktail tables, and a small stage platform combine to make the lounge an intimate yet exciting amenity to the docking pavilion.

(opposite, bottom) Brio's rustic atmosphere provides seating for eighty people. Imported tile floors, beamed ceilings, wrought-iron chandeliers, and a photomural enhance a comfortable dining experience.

PHOTOS: CHRIS BARRETT/HEDRICH BLESSING

(above) The dining room at Heaven on Seven, a Cajun Creole restaurant in Chicago, is saturated with dark stained wood shutters, floor, and crown moldings. The textured walls take on a golden glow from candles in the gilded, carved-wood chandeliers.

(opposite, top) The custom winding steel and concrete entry stair leading from the back alley directs patrons under a whimsical and colorful chandelier and into 56 West, an ultra-hip Chicago restaurant.

(opposite, bottom) An oversized mirror reflects the serene quality of the 56 West dining room.

PHOTOS: MARK BALLOGG-STEINKAMP/BALLOGG

AXIS NETWORK DESIGN CONSULTANTS SDN BHD

No client is the same—and no product wants the same environment as another. Coupled with the talent and professionalism of the Axis Network partners is the ability to solve difficult space planning challenges with fresh solutions and effective results. Axis Network is a full-service interior design practice based in Kuala Lumpur. The firm's hallmark is its ability to project a distinct identity for a client's corporate or brand image. Whether for retail clients (such as Isetan, Sogo, Metrojaya, and the Padini Group), hospitality design for Hyatt, Regent, and Radisson Hotels and the Accor Group, as well as corporate interiors, the Axis team delivers modern and relevant environments.

(top) At Cilantro in the Micasa Hotel in Kuala Lumpur, glass panels glow with the color of the green herb for which the restaurant is named. The ceiling is inspired by the woven pattern found in Malay rice packages, or *ketupat*. The central stair leads to the cigar/wine bar in the basements.

(bottom) The Trilogy Café, located in busy Bangsar, Kuala Lumpur, presents a simple yet highly textured interior. Patrons can linger over their coffee and local fare while leafing through books displayed at one end.

(opposite) At the Radisson Plaza in Kuala Lumpur, The Straits Restaurant uses the juxtaposition of random-pattern, terra-cotta floor pavers; backlit alabaster wall panels; star-shaped ceiling recesses; and neon lighting to create a fun, informal space with a Californian/Mediterranean flair.

PHOTOS: GERALD LOPEZ

(above) The dark merbau timber floor and simple, whitewashed walls of Cilantro recall materials used in old colonial townhouses. Silver-leaf panels used throughout refer to the exotic materials used in Asian jewelry and ornamentation.
PHOTO: GERALD LOPEZ

(opposite) The Haute Coiffure Salon at the Starhill Shopping Centre in Kuala Lumpur is animated by Versace-inspired, black-and white-striped wall paper and the saturated colors of the Thai silk upholstery on the Italianate chairs.
PHOTO: HILTON PHOTOGRAPHER

BERGMEYER ASSOCIATES, INC.

Bergmeyer Associates balances design with program and budget to create solutions unique to each project. A well-planned environment clearly communicates the vision of the company, inspires consumer loyalty, and makes it easy for everyone to understand a client's product and personality. Founded in 1973, Bergmeyer is a seventy-five-person, full-service architecture and interior design firm specializing in retail and food service design, housing, commercial buildings, and corporate interiors. Additional areas of expertise include image and identity analysis, prototype store design, and media technology. Bergmeyer works nationally and internationally, and currently ranks among the top ten architectural firms designing for the retail industry, as measured by a 1998 poll by *VM+SD* magazine.

(right) The renovated and expanded Boston Museum of Fine Arts' visitor services include a new museum store, restaurant, and cafeteria. The store presents a jewelry collection surrounded by textiles and decorative arts in a sophisticated, buyer-friendly environment.

(opposite) At New York City's Rockefeller Center, the dramatic floor pattern of the Commonwealth Brewing Company's star logo in copper, black, and purple marks the ground level entry to the two-level, 300-seat restaurant and bar. Images of labor and industry explore the idea of "commonwealth."

PHOTOS: CHUN Y. LAI

(below) Dick's Clothing and Sporting Goods in Columbia, Maryland, is organized into a series of specialty stores, each dedicated to a particular field of play. Hard goods and shoes encircle apparel at the core.

(opposite) At Dick's Clothing and Sporting Goods a variety of flooring types allows shoppers to test athletic footwear on authentic surfaces, such as hardwood floors for basketball and aerobic shoes, concrete for roller blades, and a track surface for running and cross-training shoes.

PHOTOS: CHUN Y. LAI

(below) In a major brand repositioning Levi Strauss chose the setting of an urban loft for a new prototype design for Dockers. Authentic elements and materials—such as raw, whitewashed beams and columns, aged wood floors, stained oak fixtures, and hand forged metal—highlight this Troy, Michigan, location.
PHOTO: CHUN Y. LAI

(right) Boston was chosen as the first North American freestanding location for AKRIS, a Swiss couturier, because of its similarity to European cities. Working with Sopha Sa Architects of Paris, a precisely detailed interior reflects and highlights the elegance of the product.
PHOTO: LUCY CHEN

BOGDANOW PARTNERS ARCHITECTS

The Bogdanow office approaches design with an attitude that gives equally high priority to comfort and function. The work is characterized by the use of rich, warm materials and colors—and frequently a surprising twist. As much if not more than large budgets, ingenuity adds a special element to give each project its own identity. Concern for the end-user is especially apparent in the firm's restaurant work. In its designs for more than forty restaurants, Bogdanow has fashioned interiors that patrons want to spend time in. They are well-lit and acoustically mellow, with unusual furnishings for interest and humor. Projects use real materials: environmentally sound woods, natural fiber textiles, and metals for warmth or accents, and as often as possible, existing elements of a room or building will be incorporated into the design.

(above) A skylight and trussed ceiling over the main dining room of Union Pacific, an elegant and serene restaurant in New York City, provides generous light by day and a glowing canopy at night.

(opposite) A simple wall of water greets diners and sets a Zen-like tone for Union Pacific.
PHOTOS: PAUL WARCHOL

(above, top) Merchants, New York uses playful colors, textures, and patterns to define the bar, restaurant, and cigar lounge.
PHOTO: PETER AARON/ESTO

(above) Plush furnishings at Merchants, New York make an upstairs lounge an intimate "living room." Gold flecks fill the cove-lit night blue sky ceiling with shimmering stars.
PHOTO: PETER AARON/ESTO

(opposite) Rain is a neighborhood Thai/Pan-Asian restaurant on New York's Upper West Side. Whimsical elements in the front bar include a Bentwood gazebo and a painted carpet runner.
PHOTO: ROBERT BLOSSER

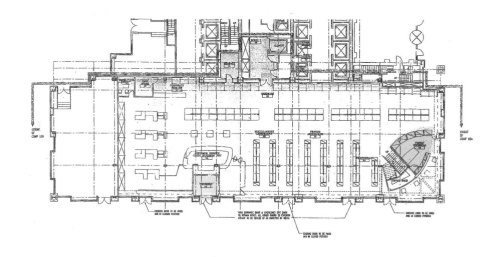

BRENNAN BEER GORMAN MONK/INTERIORS

The firm's successful and creative solutions result from a team approach that is dedicated to design excellence and technical savvy. As such, with offices in New York City, Washington, D.C., and Hong Kong, Brennan Beer Gorman Monk/Interiors is a leading force in hospitality, retail/entertainment, and corporate design. The firm has an international reputation for its wide spectrum of design styles. The range of classic, traditional interiors to imaginative, thematic environments can be seen in the restoration of the New York City's landmarked St. Regis, the World Wrestling Federation headquarters in Connecticut, the ancient Rome-inspired Caesar's Atlantic City, and the reinterpretation of the Tales of Scheherazade at the Aladdin Hotel & Casino, Las Vegas.

(right) Mixing retail with entertainment, the firm created Transporter: Movies You Ride, a simulated adventure ride in the Empire State Building. Inspired by postapocalyptic film sets, a theatrical progression of spaces was carved into the 4,500-square-foot (405-square-meter), below-grade space.
PHOTO: PAUL WARCHOL

(opposite) Comp USA's first urban store located on Manhattan's Fifth Avenue, presents the computer retailer's suburban warehouse image with an upscale look. Just inside the two-level glass façade and exposed staircase is an interior billboard, with a curved, two-level backlit logo in the company's signature red, video screens showcasing software, and two futuristic mannequins on the platform staring back at passersby. (floor plan, above)
PHOTO: PETER PAIGE

(below) The bar at the Peninsula Hong Kong echoes in darker tones the casual elegance of the hotel's restaurant. Wood paneling, dark-hued walls, and informal seating arrangements evoke the charm and comfort of an earlier era.

(right) For the hotel's casual yet elegant day-time eatery The Verandah, newly created fluted columns, decorative moldings, and cove ceiling evoke the hotel's original 1928 neoclassical symmetry and elegance. Wood ceiling fans and wrought-iron and glass chandeliers add to the period authenticity.

PHOTOS: ANTHONY P. ALBARELLO

CLODAGH DESIGN INTERNATIONAL

With the iconoclastic motto "Why Not?" Clodagh has established a global reputation for creating environments as "art to live in." Since 1983, New York City-based Clodagh Design International has pursued the ideal of "total design," with an inventive and sensitive style that involves all human senses and earthly elements, using materials that often—and unexpectedly—exploit the natural aging process to ensure low maintenance. Starting at the age of seventeen with her own fashion design company in Ireland, Clodagh moved naturally from being a leading Irish couturier to founding a leading interior and landscape design company in Spain. Cooperating with conservationists, her design addresses environmental concerns through energy-efficient housing involving solar and wind energy. Projects include retail, office, salon, and residential interiors in the U.S., Europe, and Pacific Rim. Clodagh Design Works is a licensing division encompassing the design of product, graphics, furnishings, and home accessories.

(above) An 8-foot (2.4-meter) tall layered fountain made of glass, stainless steel, and concrete marks the transition between the styling/merchandise and spa areas in the Noëlle Spa for Beauty & Wellness in Stamford, Connecticut.

(opposite) In Felissimo, an upscale New York City department store located in a turn-of-the-century townhouse, a giant leaf-shaped rug and an undulating terra-cotta-plastered display wall are a contemporary counterpoint to the century-old Rococo interior architecture.
ALL PHOTOS: DANIEL AUBRY

(above) At the entry to Felissimo, the bronze stair rail is complemented by bronze, glass, and steel jewelry display units. Two giant mirrors framed in oxidized steel are carefully placed for *feng shui* to bring positive energy into the store.

(opposite) A soaring front parlor room plastered in faded ochre with two giant Cheval mirrors provides a luxurious setting for Felissimo's eclectic fashion collection.

CREAR - JAIME BOUZAGLO

Inviting spaces designed by Jaime Bouzaglo, founder of CREAR, are often described as "seductive," "curvaceous," and "emotional." Born in Alcazar, Spanish Morocco and raised in Barcelona, he studied under Jean François Zevaco, a well-known French architect and developed his rigorous design techniques. His Mediterranean origin, influenced by the ocean and horizon, flows through his work, which includes restaurant, boutique, furniture, and product design. Bouzaglo keeps a vigilant eye on economic factors that influence design. "Society is moving away from the expensive image and viewing it as wasteful," he says. "The key is to create a sharp image, with creative, ecological materials." International notice of Bouzaglo's Montréal-based CREAR came with his designs for the widely dispersed Cerruti 1881 boutiques.

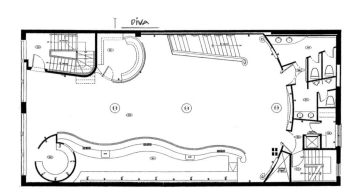

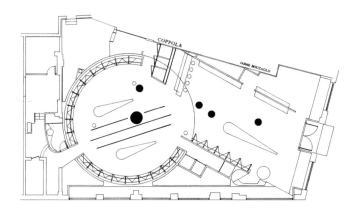

(above) Diva Discotheque, in Montréal, is dreamlike and surreal. Contrasts abound: Hot red lighting on curvaceous, futuristic (and somewhat cartoon-like) furniture is made even more sensuous by the fluid, green hues of the back bar aquarium and silver-painted fishing net draped from the ceiling. (floor plan, top)
PHOTO: PHILIPPE GUILLAUME

(opposite, top) Upon entering Bice Ristorante in Montréal, patrons are welcomed by a softly illuminated draped curtain wall, elegant seating, and warm lighting.
PHOTO: ALEX LEGAULT

(opposite, bottom) Three massive, metallic columns resembling turbines call attention to the Montréal boutique, Coppola. (floor plan, bottom)
PHOTO: PHILIPPE GUILLAUME

(left) In Montréal's Mediterraneo, rolled metal and exposed pipes become graceful forms resembling the industrial elegance of a Swatch watch.

(right) The bar in Mediterraneo is made of metal mesh with a wood top, highlighted by a backlit, glass-shelved niche.

PHOTOS: PHILIPPE GUILLAUME

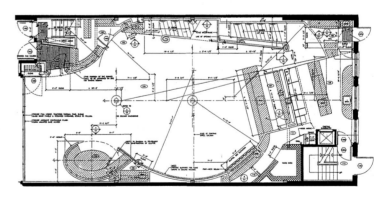

(top) At Prímadonna restaurant in Montréal, shapely golden pillars and a partial ring of delicate ceiling fixtures recall jewels worn by sophisticated women from the Golden Age of Rome. (floor plan, bottom right)

(lbottom, left) The stair rail at Prímadonna is like an ancient scroll that gracefully ends, upstairs and down, in two spirals of gypsum board.

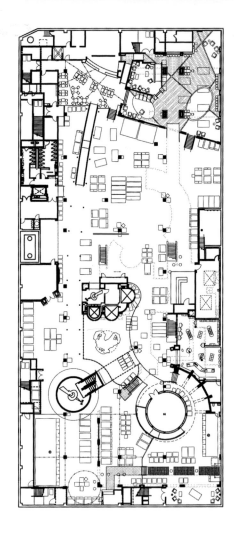

CUNINGHAM GROUP

For Cuningham Group, a successful project is a collaborative effort of architecture, interior design, show management, and construction aimed at producing exciting results through seamless project management. The 230-person Minneapolis-based Cuningham Group, with offices in Los Angeles and Phoenix, offers architecture, interior design, planning, environmental resources, visual communications, and construction services to entertainment/retail, gaming/ hospitality, education, corporate/commercial, worship/not-for-profit, assisted living, and urban markets. Over the past ten years, the firm has developed and implemented entertainment concepts for clients that include Disney, Universal Studios, Knotts Berry Farm, Rainforest Cafés, GameWorks, and Café Odyssey.

(above) At the entrance to Star Trek: The Experience in Las Vegas, ramps lead down to the retail and bar areas and up to a simulator ride based on the *Star Trek* television and movie series. (floor plan, right)

(opposite) Throughout Star Trek: The Experience, the retail area pulsates with special lighting and audio effects.

PHOTOS: GARY ZEE/OPULENCE STUDIOS

(left) The trademark Mushroom Bar at the Rainforest Café at Disney Marketplace in Lake Buena Vista, Florida, sports colorful animal rumps as barstools. A 40-foot-wide (12-meter-wide) air curtain is designed to keep cool air in and hot air and insects out.
PHOTO: DANA WHEELOCK/WHEELOCK PHOTOGRAPHY
USED BY PERMISSION DISNEY ENTERPRISES, INC.

(below) Crescendos of thunder and lightning, continuous tropical rainstorms, cool mists, and cascading waterfalls fill the Rainforest dining room. Other playful elements include animatronic animals and live parrots.
PHOTO: DANA WHEELOCK/WHEELOCK PHOTOGRAPHY
USED BY PERMISSION DISNEY ENTERPRISES, INC.

(opposite) The 16,000-square-foot (1,486-square-meter) Café Odyssey at the Mall of America in Bloomington, Minnesota, offers three distinct dining environments. The Serengeti features panoramic video projections, sound effects, and changing mood lighting. Other "destinations" at this 365-seat restaurant include the mythical lost city of Atlantis and ruins of the Incan city Machu Picchu.
PHOTO: CUNINGHAM GROUP

DESGRIPPES GOBÉ & ASSOCIATES

Comprised of interdisciplinary marketing and design teams with expertise in four key creative disciplines (brand and corporate identity, packaging, structural packaging and fixture systems, and architecture), Desgrippes Gobé is dedicated to the creation of innovative, breakthrough solutions for clients worldwide. The firm uses design to evoke an emotional response and establish a long-term bond between a company and its target audience by analyzing a brand's visual and emotional equities, and targeting the codes and cues that speak to a consumer's tastes and values. As an international brand image consultancy, Desgrippes Gobé works with dozens of companies across fashion, beauty, retail, and consumer brand industries in Europe, Asia, and the Americas, creating identity, packaging, and architectural solutions that support a client's business strategies.

(right) On the second floor, Ann Taylor customers can relax next to a double-height window that overlooks Madison Avenue and brings natural light to the upper floors.

(opposite) An elegant and refined Ann Taylor flagship store on Madison Avenue is anchored by a graceful glass and limestone staircase—the centerpiece of the 40,000-square-foot (3,716-square-meter) store that spirals up all five floors.

PHOTOS: ANDREW BORDWIN

(above) The New York City showroom for Liz Claiborne is a prototype simulation of an actual shop-in-shop retail environment. A
curved wall behind the reception area echoes the shop's radial lay-
out, and serves as a gallery for renderings of prototypical curvilinear
wood, brushed steel, and glass fixtures for Liz Claiborne department
store boutiques.

(right) Through color and graphics, three different floral motifs dis-
tinguish the Liz Claiborne career, casual, and special size subbrands.
Slipper chairs, sisal area carpets, floor lamps, and glass-topped tables
establish a feminine, residential tone.

(above, left) Reminiscent of Rockport's lighthouse logo, a splayed cylinder houses the Information Center, an interactive kiosk with information on all topics related to walking.

(above) A curved, translucent wall displays Rockport shoes on both sides, and reinforces the lighthouse motif.

(below) The Rockport Company's New York flagship store expresses the brand's "New Comfort" attitude in shoe styles. The store is divided into three lifestyle categories—performance, casual, and dress shoes—each with its own identity.

ELKUS/MANFREDI ARCHITECTS LTD.

Working with industry leaders to make their visions physically tangible, Elkus/Manfredi's designs are as diverse as its clients. Founded in 1988 by Howard F. Elkus, FAIA, RIBA, and David P. Manfredi, AIA, Elkus/Manfredi Architects has grown to more than 125 talented design professionals and continues to build upon its' outstanding project portfolio. Highly acclaimed retail work includes: the first-ever Sony Gallery on the Magnificent Mile in Chicago; the reinvention of Henri Bendel for all stores outside of New York City; prototype design for Structure, The Limited, and Express anchor pads located nationwide; the newest prototype design for HMV Records and Foot Locker; The Disney Store's signature stores at Fifth Avenue and Times Square; and other major work for Disney.

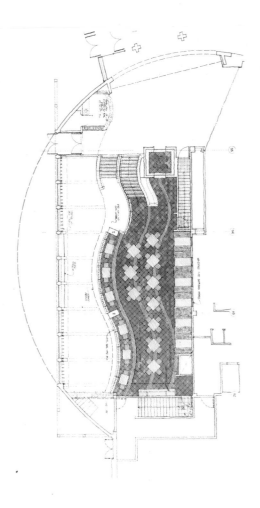

(above) The sinuous lines of pearwood display cases lead to a signature "cloud cube" portal for a special exhibition space in The Artful Hand in Boston.
PHOTO: MARCO LORENZETTI/HEDRICH BLESSING

(opposite) A series of undulating curves draw the eye through the two-level PapaRazzi's Cucina restaurant in Peabody, Massachusetts. (floor plan, right)
PHOTO: RICHARD MANDELKORN

(top) At the World of Disney Store at the Downtown Disney in Orlando, Florida, a giant Alice growing out of the White Rabbit's house is the centerpiece for plush toys in Wonderland.
PHOTO: MARCO LORENZETTI/HEDRICH BLESSING
DISNEY CHARACTERS © DISNEY ENTERPRISES, INC.
USED BY PERMISSION FROM DISNEY ENTERPRISES, INC.

(above) Magic from the Fairy Godmother's wand swirls across the ceiling of the Magic Room. The carpet design is derived from whirling breezes, cascading leaves, and shooting stars—the magic found in so many Disney movies.
PHOTO: GARY QUESADA/HEDRICH BLESSING
DISNEY CHARACTERS © DISNEY ENTERPRISES, INC.
USED BY PERMISSION FROM DISNEY ENTERPRISES, INC.

(right) Most appropriately, Captain Hook's crocodiles show off clocks in the jewel-laden Villains Room—they also begin to tick as customers draw near.
PHOTO: GARY QUESADA/HEDRICH BLESSING
DISNEY CHARACTERS © DISNEY ENTERPRISES, INC.
USED BY PERMISSION FROM DISNEY ENTERPRISES, INC.

(above) The main multimedia attraction, a twenty-four-screen video wall, sets an "urban playground" stage in a prototype Foot Locker in Watertown, Massachusetts.

(opposite) Kids Foot Locker is a larger-than-life playroom, complete with giant closets, a 9-foot-diameter (2.7-meter-diameter) basketball, oversized bikes breaking through walls, and a football portal that connects to the adjacent store.

PHOTOS: GARY QUESADA/HEDRICH BLESSING

ENGSTROM DESIGN GROUP

Whimsy and practicality come together in the work of Engstrom Design Group (EDG). Founded in 1987, the Bay Area firm is a collaboration of fifteen design, production, and administrative professionals led by principals Eric Engstrom and Jennifer Johanson. Focused on the national restaurant and hospitality market, the firm is known for its dynamic, functional spaces. There is a sense of quality and innovation in every space EDG designs that harmonizes food and restaurant concepts to enhance the overall presentation, integrating the technical complexities of restaurant design with clients' aesthetic and commercial goals. Design leadership is balanced by effective project management, and a solid track record for delivering successful projects on time and on budget.

(right) In the main dining room of the California Café near Denver, sloping redwood columns and ceiling arches support a lofty green soffit, an environment reminiscent of dining under the trees.

(opposite) The California Café pays homage to Big Tree country with a design that's heavy on wood, stone, and Rocky Mountain colors. The space is an entertaining, ever-changing journey that begins at the domed entry.

PHOTOS: ANDREW KRAMER PHOTOGRAPHY

(top) Faux river rocks surround a steel-clad fireplace, marking the casual transition from the bar to the main dining room at California Café.
PHOTO: ANDREW KRAMER PHOTOGRAPHY

(above) California Café continues through a promenade of stylized "palm tree" torchieres. Iron railings, hand-forged in an abstracted naturalistic design, enclose the intimate dining room.
PHOTO: ANDREW KRAMER PHOTOGRAPHY

(right) Another California Café Bar and Grill brings an alternative dining experience to a traditional meat-and-potatoes Chicago suburb. The environment is inspired by the architecture of nature son Frank Lloyd Wright: Polished copper chandeliers, adapted from the conical shape of Wright's Guggenheim Museum, and clusters of imposing circular dropped ceilings hightlight the dining areas.
PHOTO: WAYNE CABLE

(right) A traditional European marketplace inspired the prototype for the new in-store Nordstrom Café in Atlanta. Signage features include contemporary type-face laid over Renaissance-era food paintings framed in Art Nouveau metalwork.

PHOTOS: RION RIZZO/CREATIVE SOURCES

(below) Elaborate, old-world details—such as scalloped cherry millwork, pressed tin ceilings, and porcelain floor pavers—create an elegant, architectural backdrop for the fresh menu offerings and Nordstrom's signature retail food products.

PHOTO: RION RIZZO/CREATIVE SOURCES

(left) Located at the base of the TransAmerica Tower in San Francisco, the mezzanine ceiling in Vertigo alludes to the building's pyramidal crown. Copper-mesh screens create a shimmering moiré pattern that filters light and tones down views to the pyramid.
PHOTO: DENNIS ANDERSON

(right) The entrance to Vertigo establishes an ethereal yet architectural presence.
PHOTO: DENNIS ANDERSON

FRCH DESIGN WORLDWIDE

FRCH Design Worldwide is organized into small, highly focused studios that work closely with the client to capture the spirit of the brand and communicate its market position to the public. This collaborative approach enables the firm to bring a fresh perspective, as well as sensitivity, to each client's culture, market conditions, and new opportunities. Founded in 1968, FRCH Design Worldwide (formerly known as SDI/HTI) combines positioning and marketing strategies with the disciplines of architecture, interior design, lighting design, and graphic communications to leverage each client's brand equity in the marketplace. FRCH employs nearly 200 professionals in its Cincinnati and New York City headquarters, and is affiliated with local architects and designers in Europe, Asia, Latin America, and South Africa.

(right, top) The centerpiece of Harrah's food and party store in Las Vegas, Carnival Corner, is the coffee/juice bar, capped by an extravagant cornucopia of plastic fruit and framed by colorful metal ribbons and a floor inset with a star made of broken ceramic tiles.
PHOTO: PAUL BIELENBERG

(right, bottom) Combining entertainment, education, and retailing, Tempus Expeditions at the Mall of America in Bloomington, Minnesota, honors human ingenuity. Exemplifying man's drive to achieve is a figure running through the glass storefront, adorned with a Shakespearean quote.
PHOTO: DAN FORER

(opposite) At Tempus, human invention is celebrated by giant, foam-rubber gears suspended from the ceiling, which are reflected in the terrazzo flooring. A double arch behind the cashwrap represents humanity's architectural achievements.
PHOTO: DAN FORER

(top) In Leawood, Kansas, OshKosh B'Gosh's wholesome materials, bright colors, and playful forms contribute to a warm, upbeat selling environment. The store conveys the nostalgic appeal of an earlier, less complicated era.
PHOTO: DOUG METHOD

(above) The train station motif of OshKosh B'Gosh can be seen in the ticket booth cashwrap, the railroad track center aisle made of natural pine and red stained wood, and box car fixtures.
PHOTO: DOUG METHOD

(right) Las Vegas Harrah's Jackpot boutique features theatrical lighting, bold colors, maple wood fixtures, and terrazzo flooring embedded with chips of mirror and iridescent shells. The recurring star patterns and the curved cashwrap recall Harrah's stars-and-orbs logo.
PHOTO: PAUL BIELENBERG

(left) The World of Eddie Bauer is symbolized by a globe-like aluminum sculpture suspended in the 50-foot-high (15-meter-high) entry rotunda. The sculpture at the 28,600-square-foot (2,574-square-meter) Eddie Bauer flagship store in San Francisco rotates at a rate of one revolution per minute.

(below) A pitched roof and massive, iron-work chandeliers bring drama of scale and space to the atrium. Reflecting Eddie Bauer's roots are natural materials, including rich woods and stones from the Northwest.

(opposite) The coffee shop at Eddie Bauer's Michigan Avenue store in Chicago sports the rustic but refined style of an upscale hunting lodge. Its pitched roof, pendant lamps, leather club chairs, and whitewashed cedar plank walls create a cozy, comfortable atmosphere.

PHOTOS: PAUL BIELENBERG

FRANKE, GOTTSEGEN, COX ARCHITECTS

Erika Franke, Matthew Gottsegen, and Norman Cox all had independent practices before founding their self-named partnership firm in 1991. They each bring a diverse background in architecture, engineering, historic preservation, and design education and experience. The firm's objectives are to satisfy the need for environmentally sound and aesthetically appropriate environments, as well as to fulfill the programmatic requirements of use, construction, and economy. Franke, Gottsegen, Cox Architects has significant experience in retail and restaurant markets nationwide, collaborating with clients to establish striking and recognizable identities. The firm is expert at creating exciting visual merchandising and display environments that communicate the desired image while controlling technical and budgetary aspects.

(right) Entering Barney Greengrass at Barney's New York in Beverly Hills, one first sees the bar and a mosaic tile logo of the original New York City store—only slightly more refined (it is Beverly Hills, after all).

(opposite top) The retail/specialty food department at Barney Greengrass serves as a pathway to the open kitchen that can seat twelve for dinner at the chef's table.

(opposite bottom) Barney Greengrass has a sophisticated, but not intimidating, take-out/sit-down deli department.

PHOTOS: ALEX VERTICOFF

(above) Overall Aveda store designs may vary by site, but display techniques remain constant and familiar in every location: warm wood, glass shelving, and classic lighting fixtures.

(below) Aveda product displays, especially cosmetics, are intended to be interactive and informative; every product may be tested by a customer.

PHOTOS: ALEX VERTICOFF

(above) O' Padeiro, which means "the baker" in Portuguese, is a New York City neighborhood bakery/café the owner intends to make a nation-wide attraction.

(below) The overall design of O'Padeiro includes display elements designed to be easily replicated or adapted to any location and configuration.

PHOTOS: RICHARD EDELMAN

GENSLER

Described by *Fast Company* magazine as one of America's largest and most influential design firms, Gensler provides a full spectrum of comprehensive design and planning services. The Gensler retail group is unique in its ability to offer clients an integrated range of services that include graphic design and branding, renovation, and master planning. The firm's retail practice encompasses store/shopping center planning and design, prototype store design, packaging, identity programs, signage, and coordinating construction of chain stores. A combination of expert leadership, experience, and technology has made Gensler an international industry leader in both prototype design and the refinement of the roll-out process.

(right) At the Universal Studios Store, a retro camera icon recalls movie making in Old Hollywood, juxtaposed against an L.E.D. movie marquee announcing the latest Universal movie.

(opposite) A theatrical backdrop focusing on the process of movie making provides a framework for merchandise. Universal Studio Theme Park visitors are drawn into the store by a strategically placed video screen.

PHOTOS: NICK MERRICK/HEDRICH BLESSING

(left) The Chicago flagship store for The North Face takes on a sophisticated, rather than rustic, guise to showcase the high quality outdoor clothing and equipment. Urban modernism meets nature in a blend of stainless steel, black metal, maple and pear woods, and limestone tile.

PHOTO: JON MILLER/HEDRICH BLESSING

(below) The Experience Zone in The North Face allows customers to interact with such merchandise as sleeping bags and back packs. Textural floor changes and a climbing wall mimic and reinforce outdoor terrain and activities.

PHOTO: JON MILLER/HEDRICH BLESSING

(right) Compaq Works in Houston uses oversized photo murals to draw customers into themed areas highlighting the different places one can use a PC, from a home office or corporate work station to remote/outdoor locations. The back wall is painted in gray tones to simulate a pixel pattern.

PHOTO: STEVE HALL/HEDRICH BLESSING

(below) The geometry of playing billiards at Slick Willie's at Bayou Place in Houston is represented in shapes that descend from the ceiling. Bright colors used throughout reflect colorful pool balls.

PHOTO: JON MILLER/HEDRICH BLESSING

(above, top) Within this food wall at HomeChef in Palo Alto, California, food and the love of cooking are visually reinforced through "windows" in culinary cabinets and departmental graphics. The overall style is informal and handcrafted.
PHOTO: DAVID WAKELY

(above, bottom) The palette of the museum store at the San Francisco Museum of Modern Art acts as a neutral backdrop for brightly colored merchandise. Display cases are placed against the window wall, attracting passersby on the street.
PHOTO: CHAS MCGRATH

(right) SOMA Living is a one-stop shop with everything needed to buy a home in San Francisco's South of Market neighborhood. The space is divided into six zones designed to explain the process of home buying.
PHOTO: MARK SINCLAIR

GRID/3 INTERNATIONAL

GRID/3 International's effective teamwork creates profitable retail environments that reach target customers through brand identity and visual merchandising. An award-winning retail design firm based in Manhattan, GRID/3 takes advantage of its location and daily interaction with leading-edge ideas, firms, products, and people from around the world. Its expertise in retail design has increased profits in stores throughout the U.S., Canada, Central and South America, South Africa, and Australia. The staff's diverse cultural backgrounds and proficiency in Spanish and Portuguese, as well as English, contribute an edge when it works in countries outside the U.S. Projects have been published widely, and the firm is recognized for its strength in planning and the realization of clients' dreams.

(right) Designed in association with JGA, Inc., the Audi Park Avenue in New York City features a circular skylight that uses fluorescent light to draw attention to new models positioned on a rotating beech turntable. The dropped ceiling detail reinforces the interlocking circles of Audi's logo.

(opposite, top) German executives can meet comfortably with their U.S. counterparts around the custom-built table that seats twelve in a carpeted conference room. A glass wall provides a clear view into the Audi showroom.

(opposite, bottom) A curved beech and stainless steel reception desk in front of a custom-faceted glass wall. The recurring curve unifies the Audi logo and product with the showroom design.

PHOTOS: LASZLO REGOS

(left) Located at Christian Bernard's Store in Roosevelt Field Mall in Long Island, New York, a brass-trimmed, custom showcase of Aztec walnut veneer with minimal interior lighting and low-voltage spots overhead, adds a combination of old and new design elements into a contemporary aesthetic.
PHOTO: MICHAEL GOLD

(below) The curved, studded signature wall with an encausto plaster finish, black wrought-iron gates, and display cases with gold-etched limestone bases establish Christian Bernard's identity as a top-of-the-line French jeweler.
PHOTO: MICHAEL GOLD

(right) For Color Siete in Bogotá, Colombia, a wood-framed glass storefront and large entranceway shows a maximum of product and beckons shoppers into the store.

PHOTO: COURTESY COLOR SIETE, S.A.

(below) In Medellín, Colombia, custom-built wood tables and fixtures, discreetly branded with the Color Siete logo, form a crisp, masculine image in visual merchandising to unify the store design and product.

PHOTO: COURTESY COLOR SIETE, S.A.

HAVERSON ARCHITECTURE AND DESIGN, P.C.

Haverson Architecture and Design projects are widely recognized for combining image, craft, budget, and schedule that meet clients' expectations of achieving lasting and appropriate buildings and interiors that contribute to the public's enjoyment. Headed by partners Jay and Carolyn Haverson, the firm consists of twenty-five professionals specializing in master planning, themed entertainment, restaurant, retail, office residential, and showroom design that often includes logo and graphic design. A multicultural team contributes to the firm's versatility and ability to work in a wide range of architectural styles that draws inspiration from the past to create designs for the future.

(right) At Spiga Ristorante in Scarsdale, New York, leaning columns frame the perimeter of the main dining room, where a playful series of banquettes suggest angled shop fronts edging a piazza. Decorative finishes and colorful surfaces intensify the festive surroundings.

(opposite, top) The Motown Café at the New York Hotel and Casino in Las Vegas opens to the world's largest 46 r.p.m. record that dramatically spins overhead. The spectacular Stairway to Success is constructed of Motown's solid gold hit records.

(opposite, bottom) The warm, colorful, and dynamic main dining area of Motown Café draws upon the classic American architecture of the period—from the late 1950s to the late 1960s—visually capturing the excitement and artistic energy of the Motown sound.
ALL PHOTOS: PAUL WARCHOL PHOTOGRAPHY

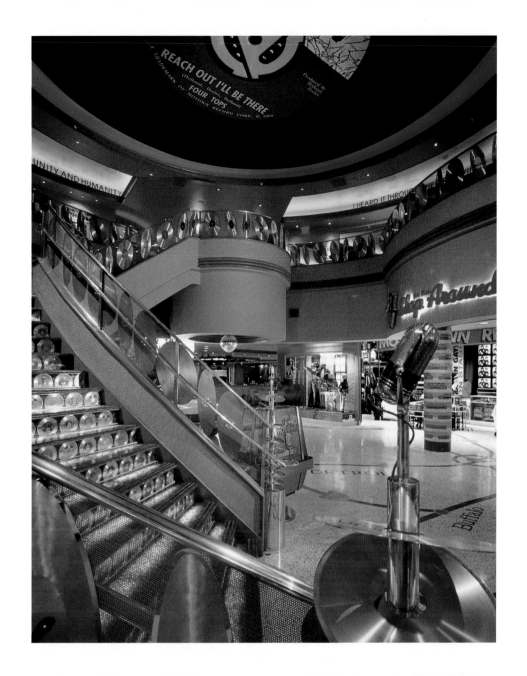

88

(left) Classical and lightly Mannerist architectural elements balance traditional yet eccentric retail fittings that characterize the Turnbull & Asser interior. The front rooms on the second and third levels are connected by a floor cut-through.

(below) Turnbull & Asser's three retail floors in New York City are designed to look as though they've always been there (two upper levels are reserved for corporate offices). Raised wood paneling with built-in custom casework is complemented with fine period furniture.

(right) The Route 66 Bar at the Harley-Davidson Café features bar stools that imitate motorcycle seats. A ceiling mural sports a map of the original Route 66.

(below) At the Harley-Davidson Café in Las Vegas, an "assembly line" of bikes journeys overhead throughout the restaurant and retail shop, disappearing into walls and floors, creating a fun, ever-changing visual attraction. The restaurant's chain-link American flag backdrop says "Made in America."

HIRSCH BEDNER ASSOCIATES

Hirsch Bedner Associates (HBA) is renowned for creating interiors that not only provide comfort, but also add a sense of drama and theater—"a stage for the guest's experience as both actor and audience." Since its founding in 1964, HBA has been a leader in establishing hospitality design as a specialty field. Its experience with hundreds of project types completed on six continents brings a unique understanding of cultural and geographical considerations, as well as financial and programmatic requirements. Affiliated companies within the firm offer specialized services ranging from art procurement and graphic and signage programs to uniform and table-top design, providing a complete turnkey approach to interiors.

(right, top) Café Blue Veranda in the Hotel Inter-Continental, Tokyo Bay, has multilevel seating surrounding a buffet. A star-filled ceiling and striking light fixtures enhance the waterfront theme.
PHOTO: JAIME ARDILES-ARCE

(right, bottom) At the Hyatt Regency Aruba, a dining area reflects the relaxed atmosphere of the idyllic resort through the use of exaggerated colors and forms related to the Caribbean.
PHOTO: DURSTON SAYLOR

(opposite) The Café Carnaval at the Westin Rio Mar Resort in Puerto Rico features brightly painted wood railings and furnishings. The patterned concrete tiles behind the buffet station reflect a traditional Caribbean-style house.
PHOTO: DURSTON SAYLOR

(top) Portofino Restaurant at the Las Vegas Sheraton Desert Inn presents a warm, contemporary Italian ambiance, rich in textures and earthy colors. Adding a sculptural element are overstuffed, curvaceous dining chairs.
PHOTO: ROBERT MILLER

(bottom) Giacometti-inspired, handmade wrought-iron drapery rods, inlaid mosaic table tops, and locally made wicker chairs (and impressive views of the Grand Canal) contribute to the relaxed atmosphere of La Cucina at the Hotel Europa & Regina in Venice.
PHOTO: JAIME ARDILES-ARCE

(above) In one of two dining rooms at Ho Wan, a five-star restaurant in the Sheraton Desert Inn, curved banquettes of plush teal mohair follow the shape of the circular room. The silver-leafed domed ceiling and sheered walls upholstered in gold add warmth and texture.

PHOTO: ROBERT MILLER

IIDA SINGAPORE PTE. LTD.

Under the leadership of founders Benteo Gineva, ASID, IIDA, and Benedict Chung B.H., the versatile and close-knit firm undertakes a variety of projects, large and small, with passion and professionalism. Knowing that clients must benefit from environments in which they live and work, design solutions are achieved by combining the spirit of artistic creativity with the realities of budget, function, and schedule. Founded in 1992, IIDA Singapore is a young and dynamic interior design consultancy with associate offices in Taiwan, Shanghai, and Vienna. IIDA Singapore evolves with its clients in this ever-changing world, and its best design has not yet been created.

(above) At the Kublai Khan Restaurant in Singapore's Park Mall Shopping Centre, chefs perform within private "dining tents," each secluded by ancient Mongolian ironwork.

(opposite) The entrance to Kublai Khan Restaurant hints that there is an exotic dining experience waiting inside.
ALL PHOTOS: BERNARD KOH

(right) The Ninth Street Pub/Disco in suburban Taiwan celebrates the music and psychedelic lighting of the American rock-and-roll era.

(below) Enhanced by backlit seascape ceiling forms, the Coral and Shell Club at Boat Quay in Singapore seductively transforms a narrow, prewar shop into a tranquil and serene environment.

(opposite) Images of Elvis and Marilyn, among other pop icons, blend with lighting—and loud music—to make the Ninth Street Pub an escape from the daily urban stress in Taiwan.

By Roy Lichtenstein

INTERNATIONAL DESIGN GROUP, INC.

Worldwide, design standards are constantly evolving and projects are becoming more diverse than ever. Understanding that good design directly impacts profitability, the International Design Group (IDG) assists developers and retailers in establishing successful identities in the highly competitive international marketplace. Since 1972, IDG has offered specialized planning and design services to retail, hospitality, themed entertainment, and shopping center developers around the world. Knowledge, expertise, fresh talent, and the latest technological advances keep the Toronto-based studio at the forefront of commercial design.

(right) Athletic attributes such as fluidity, grace, and strength describe the interior of Runners' Choice, a specialty running wear store in Toronto. Even the signage and graphics are motivating.
PHOTO: ROBERT BURLEY/DESIGN ARCHIVE

(opposite) Now going to the movies is as much fun as watching them! Bold graphics and architecture, glossy materials, and bursts of riotous color make Famous Players Silver City multiplex in Canada a wondrous, animated fantasyland.
PHOTO: RICHARD JOHNSON/INTERIOR IMAGES

(right) In Philadelphia, glass envelops the restored grandeur of the historically classic Bailey, Banks & Biddle store, providing a perfect backdrop for Zales' fine jewelry and accessories.
PHOTO: MATT WARGO PHOTOGRAPHY

(below) Forgoing stark metal shelves and cold, institutional interiors, Bottle Your Own sets a new standard for the Liquor Control Board of Ontario, a chain of government retail enterprises. Instead, warm colors and materials and bold graphics make this an inviting, self-serve spirits store.
PHOTO: ROBERT BURLEY/DESIGN ARCHIVE

(opposite) Classic and contemporary elements unite in the 45,000-square-foot (4180.5-square-meter) La Maison Simons department store in Québec City. A magnificent 38-feet-high (11.6-meter-high) frescoed dome crowns Ionic columns and arches.
PHOTO: ROBERT BURLEY/DESIGN ARCHIVE

JGA, INC.

For retail design, JGA (formerly Jon Greenberg & Associates) believes that successfully bringing a creative idea to reality requires the integration of strategic clarity, competitive and market awareness, conceptual innovation, and a strong business sense. As part of the client's project team, JGA motivates the creative process by provoking ideas and solutions, and facilitating the management process through comprehensive design, scheduling, budgeting, and implementation, resulting in increased consumer interaction and satisfaction. The firm offers a diverse menu of services: market and design strategy, conceptual positioning, visual communication design, logo/brand identity, design and architectural development and implementation, construction, administration, roll-out programs, and fixturing/furniture/materials procurement.

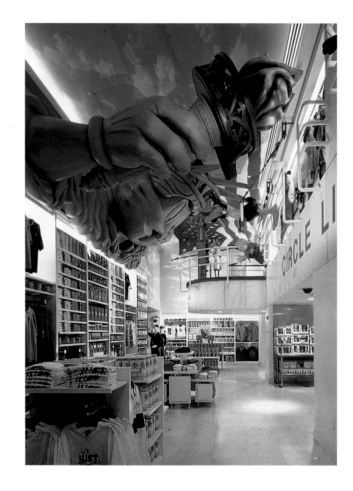

(right) At the Warner Bros. Fifth Avenue flagship store, part of the third floor ceiling was removed to create a two-story space, where an enormous Bugs Bunny acting as the Statue of Liberty greets an NYC sightseeing boat.

(opposite, top) The private party room for receptions, press conferences, and birthday celebrations exhibits a wall mural of Warner Bros. superheroes in the Pop Art style of artist Roy Lichenstein.

(opposite, bottom) The two-story Warner Bros. Wacky Acme Labs offers interactive games and a funnel-like plasma display.

PHOTOS: SCOTT FRANCES

(right) A blue glow looms over Café Site, replicating the color emitted from a computer screen. Freestanding pods serve as computer workstations. The black vinyl floor embedded with glitter reflects the metallic finishes used throughout the café.
PHOTO: SUNG YI YONG

(below) Among the twenty-plus stores JGA designed in a subterranean mall excavated beneath Samsung Corporation headquarters in Seoul, Korea, the spaceage cybercafe Café Site offers shoppers a respite to enjoy refreshments while they surf the Internet.
PHOTO: SUNG YI YONG

(opposite, top) Brookstone's flagship prototype on Manhattan's West 57th Street presents a universally branded identity for its products. Lifestyle categories are further delineated by micro-marketing pods.
PHOTO: LASZLO REGOS

(opposite, bottom) In contrast to a typically linear music store, Camelot Music's highly flexible fixturing, advanced graphics, and template lighting offer the feel of a great architectural environment, encouraging shoppers to linger in the Great Lakes Mall Store in Ohio.
PHOTO: MICHAEL HOUGHTON

(left) The openness of the Giorgio Beverly Hills flagship is aimed at bringing the outdoors in and the indoors out for a perfect California experience. Pigmented plaster walls are a sun-drenched Tuscan palette of yellows and creams.
PHOTO: STEPHEN GRAHAM

(below) The restored Madison Avenue flagship brownstone provides a new brand presence for an American icon—the Elizabeth Arden Red Door Salon & Spa. The first floor is both a retail environment and the foyer to the renowned salon (designed by Clodagh) on the levels above.
PHOTO: LASZLO REGOS

(opposite) This Fossil watch store at a mall in Columbus, Ohio, emphasizes the hip, nostalgic, and unique image shoppers have come to recognize. The interior is stylishly sleek in its warm ecru palette with rich cherry and maple veneers.
PHOTO: LASZLO REGOS

PLANUNGSGRUPPE JÖHNK

With the goal to make every project absolutely unique, there is no specific Planungsgruppe Jöhnk style, but rather an individual character and sense of time, place, and function. Regardless of the size of a project, the designers search for an overriding theme to capture the emotions of the present that will endure into the future. Established in 1984 by Peter Jöhnk, the firm offers a full range of interior design services, project management, and corporate identity consulting, with the main focus in hotel, retail, leisure, entertainment, and restaurant design. With a staff of more than thirty-five, Jöhnk is headquartered in Hamburg and maintains offices in Rosenheim, Germany, and Zurich, Switzerland.

(right) The express service in Nordsee in Frankfurt has video screens set into the floor. Steel-legged tables are topped with artificial blue stone, playing off the natural stone garden under the staircase.

(opposite) Bistro Blechnapf carries through the industrial aesthetic of its location, a landmarked building in Neumünster, Germany. The terrazzo-topped bar is faced with backlit aluminum panels.
ALL PHOTOS: CHRISTIAN KERBER

(right) The brick and antique oak bar at the FEC II Brewery in Stuttgart wraps around glistening copper brewing tanks. The barstools are upholstered in cowhide.

(below) The sweetness of youth and Old World charm abounds in the Stuttgart Candy Shop. Antique furnishings, pastel colors, hand-painted wall trim, and floor tiles in a windmill pattern recall simpler times.

(opposite, top) The urban entertainment/retail center FEC II in Stuttgart, Germany, presents a lively, animated interior. The black matte steel ceiling in the music store allows the merchandise to stand out against the brightly-colored, multi-shaped display units.

(opposite, bottom) SWF 3 Rockcafé is an American-style restaurant in FEC II, complete with diner-like seating. The "elk" chairs reflect the logo of the SWF3 radio station. Table tops resembling theatrical shipping cases and authentic stage lighting add to the rock-and-roll ambiance.

SFJONES-ARCHITECTS

Instilled by founder Stephen Francis Jones, AIA, the firm's philosophy is to integrate a client's needs and concepts and unique attributes of a site and structure with innovative, and timeless, design solutions. Everything from structural and mechanical requirements to lighting and furnishings are designed and coordinated by the firm. The studio is more in tune with an artisan workshop than a typical architectural office. SFJones' projects are notable for the use of unconventional materials, sculptural design elements, and the careful articulation of space. The attention to detail is reflected in the numerous subprojects that are created between designer and master craftsmen, ranging from glass blowers to ornamental iron fabricators and woodworkers to stonemasons.

(above) The colorful and whimsical interior of La Maison du Cigar glows brightly on Beverly Hill's tony Rodeo Drive. Designed in collaboration with the French firm Bonetti & Garouste, it is a departure from traditional English décor usually associated with cigar shops. (floor plans, right)

(opposite) Ornamental grill work and glass define La Maison du Cigar's walk-in humidors on both levels. The gilded, gold-leaf railings and patterned carpet were fabricated in France.
PHOTOS: ANTHONY PERES

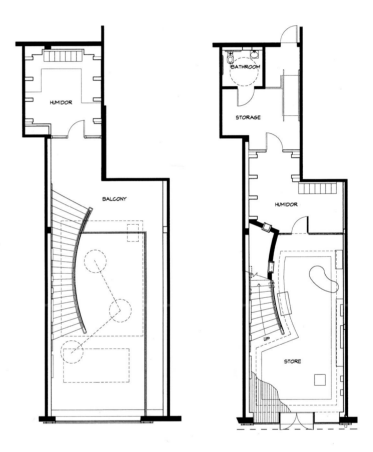

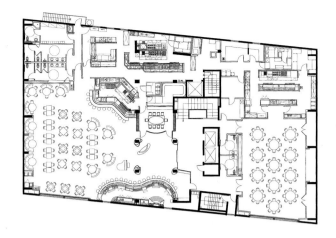

(right) At David Paul's Diamond Head Grill at the Colony Surf Hotel in Honolulu, sliding glass doors open to a view of Diamond Head. Mahogany trim and cast aluminum handrails reinforce the curvilinear elements of restaurant's interior.

(below) Undulating curves appear throughout David Paul's, from the border between the bamboo floor and carpet and the shape of the bar, to the ribbon track light and the embossed copper hood at the appetizer bar. (floor plan, top)

PHOTOS: DAVID FRANZEN

(below) The Hump is a sushi bar/Japanese restaurant located atop the Santa Monica Airport in California. The sandblasted glass mural of the Himalayan mountain range hints at the story behind the name. The Hump is accentuated by radial mahogany beams, sea grass ceiling, and random bamboo thatching. (floor plan, left)

(bottom) Rather than typical Japanese décor, The Hump's distinctive furnishings from India and Indonesia reinforce the theme of a Himalayan outpost: a distressed wood chest converted to the maitre d' stand, ornamental grills as front doors, and teak and leather bar stools. Aluminum fisherman's lanterns and ceiling fans resembling propellers add a nautical/aeronautical sparkle to the seaside airport eatery.
PHOTOS: ANTHONY PERES

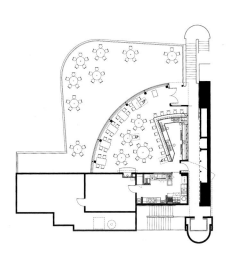

LEMAY MICHAUD ARCHITECTURE DESIGN

The basic architectural and design values attached to projects by Lemay Michaud are hospitality, the clarity and readability of designed spaces, user comfort, and respect for the built and natural surroundings. For a client, these values translate in economic terms into increased market value, longevity, efficiency (including facilitating work and communication), versatility, and reduced maintenance and operating costs. The broad experience of Lemay Michaud has won the continued loyalty of private and public sector clients ranging from hotel and restaurant chains and real estate agencies to financial, insurance, and public institutions. A multi-disciplinary staff specializing in architecture, interior design, and food services planning is particularly well-suited to restore and renovate both historic and modern buildings to accommodate hotels, restaurants, and retailers.

(above) The renovation of Bistango, in Québec City, makes it now as busy at noon as it was for dinner. The palette was inspired by a French flower market—a soft yellow, lustrous deep reds, and a rich, dark blue.

(opposite) At the back of Bistango a wall covered in alternating clear and tinted diamond-shaped mirrors animates and opens up the room.

ALL PHOTOS: JEAN BEAULIEU

(left) Among several theatrical gestures in Montréal's Pointe des Amérique is a sculptural curtain that adds to the mystery of a walled-up doorway.

(below) Connected to Pointe des Amérique is Bar Biloxi, an inviting neighborhood bar.

(right) The renovation of Café du Monde transformed one of Old Québec City's most popular eateries into a classic Parisian bistro. Lighting, mirrors, and large streetfront windows make the space vibrate with rich, shifting light.

(below) Québec City's Bistango's streetfront window panes are a counter-balance to the mirrored wall.

LIEBER COOPER ASSOCIATES

Lieber Cooper Associates (LCA) offers its clients a unique integration of services that benefit by drawing from the diverse skills of a multi-disciplined and multi-talented staff. Seeking to find new ways to synthesize beauty and function, LCA employs a wide range of creative approaches and styles to achieve a smoothly executed and aesthetically intriguing end result for every assignment. Underlying each project process is a search for the future—what burgeoning trends can be identified and what solutions can be dreamed. LCA is an architectural, interior design, and environmental graphics firm headquartered in Chicago. In an effort to blend multiple areas of expertise, the firm was created in 1998 by the merger of two highly respected design practices, Lieber Architects, Inc. and Marve Cooper Design.

(right) The Big Downtown in the landmarked Palmer House recaptures Chicago in the heyday of long-distance rail travel. Period props stock the overhead luggage racks, and well-known rail destinations adorn partitions.

(opposite) Dramatically juxtaposed classical and contemporary forms mirror the cuisine of Café Spiaggia in Chicago. The gallery-like setting links past and present, combining fifteenth-century frescoes from the *Camera degli Sposi* in Mantua with contemporary Italian artifacts.
ALL PHOTOS: MARK BALLOGG, STEINKAMP/BALLOGG

(top) The main dining room of the Palmer House Hilton in Chicago is skirted and crossed by illuminated elevated trains and architectural detailing alluding to the city's well-known riverfront esplanade. A replica of the famous Chicago Theater marquee frames the display kitchen.

(bottom) Stir Crazy in Northbook, Illinois, offers a warm and comfortable social setting where playfully layered elements are finished in natural materials and exotic painted textures. Whimsical custom lighting fixtures cast a soft, amber glow.

(right) Fulton's Crab House, a 750-seat riverboat restaurant at Pleasure Island at Walt Disney World Resort near Orlando, Florida, features the Stone Crab Lounge, a showcase of commissioned fishery art and artifacts that pay tribute to the commercial fishing industry.
USED BY PERMISSION FROM DISNEY ENTERPRISES, INC.

DAVID LING
ARCHITECTS

Informed by his multi-cultural background (raised in the U.S., studies in Germany, and an umbilical link to China), David Ling honed his architectural, design, and artistic skills working with several international firms such as Richard Meier & Partners and I.M. Pei & Partners, working on projects in the U.S., Germany, The Netherlands, and Hong Kong. Focusing on the integration of space, light, form, and texture, David Ling Architects has developed a material vocabulary with the "desire to choreograph opposites in a dance of tension," adaptable to varied sites, budgets, and programs. Characteristic of his design direction is the use of interlocking spaces and forms articulated by a crafted use of materials. Based in New York, Berlin, and Cologne, Ling's work in the U.S. ranges from museums, galleries, stores and offices to high-end residential projects for patrons of the arts. German clients include larger scale commercial, institutional, and theater spaces.

(right) The Philosophy Boutique for Alberta Ferretti, in New York City's SoHo, is a fluid Renaissance theater. The glass storefront presents a three-story view onto the "stage" animated and illuminated, day and night, by skylights and theatrical lighting.

(opposite) Taking upstage center at Philosophy is a zigzag stairway sandwiched between two layers of cotton scrim and silhouetted in front of a sandblasted glass wall. Daylight from one of two skylights creates a luminous, almost ethereal textural contrast between the wall and scrim in the stairwell.
PHOTOS: TODD EBERLE

(below) Center stage of Philosophy is a sloped glass floor lit from below through gently cascading water.
PHOTO: TODD EBERLE

(bottom) In the Apollo Bar in Cologne, Germany, juxtaposing warm wood and metal in a dialogue between gentle curves and hard edges results in an intriguing, intimate environment. The bar, clad in cherry wood, takes on the shape of the inside of a ship's hull. Opposite is a lead-clad, "folded" wall.
PHOTO: HELMUT STAHL

(right) The interior of a black funnel form that from the street visually dissects the mezzanine floor in Philosophy, becomes a graceful, ornamental niche.
PHOTO: TODD EBERLE

JOHN LUM ARCHITECTURE

John Lum has developed a signature style that combines the rationality and rigorous detailing of Modernism with the warmth and humanism of artistic intuition. He believes in purity of form and using materials honestly, combining them in inventive ways to create a rich palette of unusual colors, forms, and textures. Compositionally beautiful, each project creates a personal experience that reflects a client's unique personality. Lum established his San Francisco-based firm in 1994, after seven years as a principal designer at Reid and Tarics Associates, focusing on corporate, educational, and institutional facilities. Lum is best known for his award-winning, high-end, high-image retail and hospitality interiors. He is also very involved in creating innovative residential projects ranging from single family homes to affordable housing complexes.

(right) Upholstered organic-shaped banquette backs complement the rhomboid maple table tops, vivid blue and green seat cushions, and the orange and yellow striped walls of the dining balcony at Paradis in Palo Alto, California.

(opposite) Concrete and steel mixed with existing antique wood-work create a hip environment for Paradis transforming a dowdy Irish pub into a sizzling jazz club featuring modern California cuisine.
ALL PHOTOS: SHARON RISEDORPH

(left) At Asia SF, a San Francisco restaurant and nightclub, entry curtains and a sheet metal screen give way to a surreal Asian environment replete with mythological references to dragons and exotic locales.

(below) Dr. Jimmy Fong Optometry is based on the ellipse of an eye; a curved display wall acts as a billboard to the street, a dynamic gesture accentuated by striated walls. A suspended "eye" overhead provides uplighting. (floor plan, below)

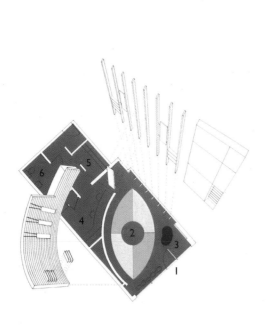

(right) An ash veneer cube masks the restroom in Urban Eyes Optometry in San Francisco, California, while providing storage and seating. Lag bolts are used to display glasses, and a structural column features hand prints of the optometrists.

(below) At a mere 450 square feet (40.5 square meters), Urban Eyes uses a triangulated, telescopic geometry that beckons passersby into the boutique. Layering of rich materials such as stained ash veneer, bas relief plaster, and painted surfaces add depth and texture.

MICHAEL MALONE ARCHITECTS, INC.

Michael Malone Architects, Inc. (MMA) takes a research-oriented approach to design that focuses on organizing a store to optimize the presentation of merchandise and customer flow while maximizing the opportunity for flexible display and surprises. Most of MMA's creative work is for first-time retail concepts, often for major corporations using retail stores as a vehicle to increase market awareness of a brand. MMA executes details that include lighting and fixture design, props, and icons. The firm also provides full environmental and informational graphics that allow a store to have many signature elements as integral elements of the design. For purposes of construction and fabrication, MMA has access to architectural registration in all fifty states and many foreign countries.

(right) The center rotunda of Voyagers: The Travel Store in Plano, Texas. Voyagers contains the service and cashwrap desk, and, of course, a column of clocks showing the time around the world.
PHOTO: STEVE VAUGHAN PHOTOGRAPHY

(opposite) The floor of Shell Oil's Encompass Store in Houston sports a tile map of western Pennsylvania, birthplace of the oil industry. A toy-sized, 1912 tank truck and historic pumps are stocked with merchandise.
PHOTO: JUD HAGGARD PHOTOGRAPHY

(top) A decorative wood trellis covers the cashwrap counter and creates a focal centerpiece for the Blue Canoe, a gift and garden store in Seattle, Washington. The maple floor adds the metaphor of a rural porch or verandah.
PHOTO: PATRICK BARTA PHOTOGRAPHY

(above) Multimedia towers encourage customers to browse the Discovery Channel CD-ROM and other interactive and on-line products at the Galleria in Houston, Texas. Video monitors above allow other customers to watch the interaction.
PHOTO: JUD HAGGARD PHOTOGRAPHY

(right) The sophisticated environment for the Discovery Channel store uses slate, wood, and powder-coated metal to house large format video screens, an aquarium, and movable display fixtures.
PHOTO: JUD HAGGARD PHOTOGRAPHY

PATRICK MCBRIDE COMPANY

Grand ideas are one thing…. It is quite another to bring those wonderful concepts to successful realization. That is why the McBride Company team consists of such a wide array of eclectic talents—architects, set designers, writers, art directors, producers, interior designers, and project managers. A spirit of boundless imagination and capable, consistent delivery has propelled the company to the forefront of the fast-moving marketplace in destination entertainment, retail, food and beverage, and themed attractions. With an unwavering focus on success and the quality of the guest experience, the firm's roster of projects is as broad as one could imagine. The outcome of the McBride Company's work is best known to the millions of people who have visited its attractions, malls, restaurants, shops, museums, and other fascinating environments.

(right) At Coco Marina a sense of outdoor dining is created inside New York City's World Financial Center lobby by the use of free floating awnings, French doors, and a more casual selection of furnishings. Shades of white with accents of cobalt blue create a mood of casual elegance, a trademark of Coco Pazzo restaurants.

(opposite) A grand staircase architecturally and visually connects the multiple levels of Tuscan Square at New York City's Rockefeller Center. Kiln-treated handrails, custom-iron work, a preserved cypress from Tuscany, and exotic displays grace the descent.
PHOTOS: ROB GRAY

(above) This Hard Rock Café has been uniquely crafted to capture the essence of Key West's historic Victorian architecture while staying true to Hard Rock's image as the citadel of rock-and-roll.
PHOTO: EDUARDO GALLIANI

(right) Jimmy Buffet represents an adventurous yet laid back way of life. His Margaritaville store in Charleston, South Carolina, with its masts, sailcloth, and weathered woods, marries both the Buffet lifestyle and the city's pirate-laden history.
PHOTO: ALTERMAN STUDIOS

(opposite) An eclectic collection of signature products, Margaritaville "parrot head" merchandise is displayed in a beautifully restored wooden Chris Craft "moored" precariously against the original brick of the building. The weathered lyrics of a Buffet song wash like a wave along the wall.
PHOTO: ALTERMAN STUDIOS

JORDAN MOZER & ASSOCIATES

The signature design of Jordan Mozer & Associates (JMA) is fantasy and intrigue without being repetitive. While the thirty-person, Chicago-based firm is best known for its entertainment, restaurant, and nightclub projects worldwide, it is also accomplished in retail facilities and corporate and industrial buildings. The JMA team includes architects, interior designers, sculptors, painters, and fabricators that has allowed it to develop design/build methods to create highly customized projects with the ability to control quality, pricing, and schedule. Examples of recent and ongoing commissions include components of WDI Disney Quest in Orlando, Florida, and several venues in Steve Wynn's Bellagio (including a whimsical store for Cirque de Soleil). JMA recently introduced a line of furnishings for hotels, clubs, and restaurants at the Trend Hotel Convention in Hanover, Germany, that will most likely become mainstay products of the hospitality industry.

(above) Surf 'n Turf, in Matsuyama, Japan, plays with the idea of *Manga*, or Japanese cartoons—everything is pudgy and rounded like cartoon forms. Ceiling fixtures recall sea urchins; bar stools, the back bar display, and even the custom beer mugs have little feet; and the sconces are "fire-breathing" dragons.

(opposite) Surf 'n Turf combines American and Japanese popular cultures (and cuisines). At the entrance to Surf 'n Turf's private dining rooms, the first newel posts stand at attention and the second ones "bow" to patrons ascending the stairs.
PHOTOS: TAKEICHI

(below) The main dining room at Surf 'n Turf has *tako* (octopus) columns and lighting fixtures. The chair backs are waving cartoon hands.

PHOTO: TAKEICHI

(bottom) The copper portal leading to the Cypress Club's private dining room is puffed up, like an old airplane wing. Above, and encircling the Chicago restaurant, is a Thomas Hart Benton-style mural of Monterey cypress trees and Napa Valley vineyards.

PHOTO: KINGMOND YOUNG

(right) The Cheesecake Factory in Chicago is an amalgam of motifs inspired by cheesecake filling, rock-and-roll (the owner is a former drummer), Asian art (the owner's passion), and turn-of-the-century European cafés.

PHOTO: DAVID CLIFTON

142

NBBJ

In 1943, four Seattle architects (Naramore, Bain, Brady, and Johanson) joined forces to design a total support community for one of the nation's major naval shipyards. The collaboration was successful; the partners, compatible. All agreed that by pooling their talents and resources they could create the consummate architectural practice: a multi-specialty firm dedicated to providing quality design and superior service to its clients. Based on the studio concept under which NBBJ was founded, the retail concepts studio was established twelve years ago in response to the marketplace. James Adams, principal in charge and founder of the studio, has assembled a talented and diverse group of retail design professionals. Their ability to look at the customer experience and translate it back to a successful solution for clients gives the studio a strong competitive edge, with a strong portfolio of work for leading retailers.

(above) Although a prototype for a roll-out of the Mr. Rags brand, the design for the Bellevue, Washington, store does not use standard retail materials and equipment, but rather inexpensive and readily available materials that a teenager might use to outfit his/her hangout.
PHOTO: TOM OGLE

(opposite, top) Free-standing dressing rooms in Mr. Rags are clad in panels cut from fifty-five gallon steel drums; bare light bulbs on extension cords dangle from the exposed ceiling grid; and walls and floors feature hot rolled steel panels.
PHOTO: STEVEN KEATING

(opposite, bottom) The Mr. Rags cashwrap sparkles with woven wire mesh, stainless steel, and ceramic sockets with bare bulbs.
PHOTO: STEVEN KEATING

(above) Dramatically different from its original blue neon look, Mr. Rags uses raw and "found" materials to create a store with a lot of attitude. Recycled diner stools sit in front of a custom stainless-steel cabinet.

PHOTO: STEVEN KEATING

(left) The Puget Consumers Co-op (PCC) in Seattle is one of the nation's largest cooperatively owned natural and organic grocer. Various preparation areas such as the free-standing display counter in Bulk Foods, help staff to interact with customers.
PHOTO: PAUL WARCHOL

(below) The PCC's wide circulation paths and natural lighting create a sense of an outdoor roadside market. A steel canopy sporting pendant lamps made of kitchen colanders identify the produce area.
PHOTO: PAUL WARCHOL

ROCKWELL GROUP

New York City-based Rockwell Group, with a current staff of almost 200, is best known for architectural projects for The Walt Disney Company, Cirque du Soleil, and Radio City Music Hall. Recent projects include the renovation of Manhattan's W Hotel, Michael Jordon NYC, and the Dining Concourse in Grand Central Terminal, a permanent home for Cirque du Soleil in Orlando, Florida, and a new theater for the Academy of Motion Picture Arts and Sciences.

(above) In New York City, large tatami mats hang on Next Door Nobu's straw-colored Venetian plaster wall, setting off the vibrant colors and patterns of the plush, quilted banquette cushions. Traditional Japanese fishing baskets are used as suspended ceiling fixtures.

(opposite) Next Door Nobu features a glowing "sake temple" that masks a service bar (the bottles were emptied by the patrons next door).
ALL PHOTOS: PAUL WARCHOL

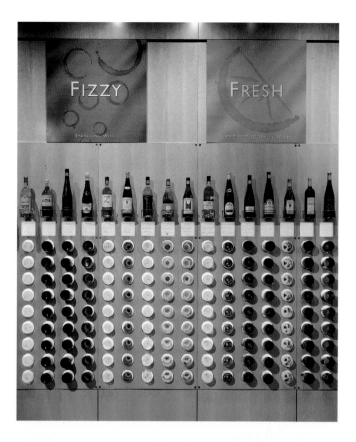

(top) A new concept in wine retailing is the prototype in New York City for a national chain for Best Cellars. The streamlined design of Best Cellars allows the wines to be the stars of the show. Bottles are displayed in backlit cabinetry, creating a colorful stained glass effect.

(above) Best Cellars offers 100 wines for under $10, organized in categories such as "soft," "smooth," and "sweet" instead of grape type or region.

(right) In Manhattan's ever-popular Nobu, "trees" made from birch tree trunks, rusted steel plates, and solid ashwood branches also serve as lighting columns. "Chopsticks"—framed stools bask in the green glow of backlit green onyx sushi bar.

(right) Rich mahogany woodwork and blown glass lighting fixtures of the two-level Payard Patisserie and Bistro in New York City evoke the sense of an established neighborhood pastry shop inspired by European cafés of the Belle Epoch.

(below) The glamour of Monkey Bar, a famed New York City hot spot in the 1930s and 1940s, has been restored and enhanced. Original monkey sconces and a Vela monkey mural have been restored, while new barstools are whimsical "martini olives."

(opposite) The Baang palette is a fusion of colors inspired by exotic spices like ginger root yellow, chili pepper red, and leek green. In Chinese, *baang* means to bind or tie together. In Aspen, Colorado, Baang restaurant blends Asian and French cuisines in an atmosphere that combines a hip, cosmopolitan sensibility with an earthy, casual one. The ceiling is a series of "clouds" imprinted with Aspen leaves; the clouds rest on glowing mica columns.

RITA ST. CLAIR ASSOCIATES

Using color, form, texture, and light, Rita St. Clair design teams fabricate and subtly orchestrate many diverse elements to shape and create enduring spaces. Integral to all of this is access to a worldwide network of commercial resources and craftsmen, and an inventory of many unusual and distinctive furnishings and accessories especially appropriate to large public spaces, allowing the delivery of unique, cost-effective design solutions. Rita St. Clair Associates has an international reputation for designing elegant, contemporary, and adaptively restored spaces through over thirty years of experience with restaurant, hospitality, country club, office, educational, daycare, health-care, religious, condominium, and residential projects. Interior design must not only be beautiful, but also responsive to the client's program and budget, and ultimately, welcomed by the end user.

(right) A sense of a Southern environment is created in the cocktail lounge at Charleston, a Baltimore restaurant, through the use of etched glass panels that introduce a palm motif also used in the carpeting, lighting fixtures, and partitions.

(opposite) Charleston's open kitchen and airy dining room epitomize Southern hospitality and complement the elegant Southern cuisine of Chef Cindy Wolf.
PHOTOS: GORDON BEALL

(below) The Polo Grill in Baltimore features freestanding tables in the center, surrounded by perimeter banquettes upholstered in a combination of paisley and faux animal skin ultrasuede.
PHOTO: MAXWELL MACKENZIE

(bottom) The Peabody Court Restaurant/Conservatory in Baltimore emulates the legendary elegance of turn-of-the-century Parisian restaurants, replete with ornate ironwork and lighting fixtures, and a Joseph Sheppard mural behind the bar.
PHOTO: MIKE HALES

(right) Subdued, varied lighting and the architectural nature of the wood racks in Charleston make the wine area a warm, intimate space.
PHOTO: GORDON BEALL

SHEA ARCHITECTS, INC.

Every project begins with a fresh approach to the distinctive needs and overall goals of each client. Employing innovative and creative design solutions, Shea Architects provides high-quality services that maximize long-term performance. The firm uses the latest technology in CAD (computer-aided design) and SheaLink, an interactive Internet design process. These tools provide greatly expanded information gathering and retrieval capabilities, allowing design teams to produce highly-detailed renderings and reports on a more timely and cost-efficient basis. Shea Architects, with approximately sixty employees, specializes in restaurant/hospitality, retail, entertainment, corporate, and historical preservation design.

(right) The Cup, a prototype for a coffee/grab-and-go kiosk for the University of Minnesota, uses colorful, dimensional graphics to present a festive and memorable image.

(opposite) The new Goodfellow's in Minneapolis is derived from authentic parts (held in storage for years and relocated here) of the original nightspot. Goodfellow's spider web wine display is a mechanical grille from the original 1929 space.
PHOTOS: GREG PAGE

(right) Influenced by the black vitrolite wainscot surrounding the restaurant, Goodfellow's bar features a backlit, glue-chipped glass bar top supported by custom chromed brackets.

(below) The main dining room at Goodfellow's offers an expansive view of vintage Art Deco details, many from the original 1929 interior, transported to a contemporary downtown location.

PHOTOS: GREG PAGE

(right) Tejas, in Edina, Minnesota, presents a welcoming, neighbor-hood atmosphere imbued with a Santa Fe style. The heart of Tejas is counter seating facing the open kitchen. The proximity of customers to chefs animates the space.
PHOTO: STEPHEN BERGERSON PHOTOGRAPHY

(below) The walls and ceilings of Famous Dave's, in Forest Lake, Minnesota, are filled with antique Southern country shack decor and tin roofing, bringing a rustic character and charm to the interior.
PHOTO: STUART LORENZ

EARL SWENSSON ASSOCIATES, INC.

Earl Swensson Associates' hallmark is integrating sophisticated architecture, design, and technology into "human-centered" environments. The Wildhorse Saloon is an outstanding example of the firm's ability to coordinate, within one facility, dining, production, broadcasting, entertainment, and retail activities. Founded in 1961 and currently staffed with more than 160 professionals, the firm provides services in architecture, interior design, master planning, and space planning. Projects range from hotel/convention centers, restaurants, corporate and speculative office facilities, retail, and public buildings to educational health-care facilities, comprehensive and senior living residential communities, and headquarters for religious and industrial groups.

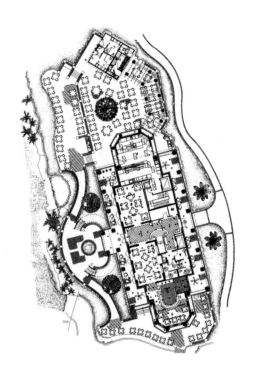

(above) Beauregard's downstairs library, with a fireplace and wine display as focal points, offers a cozy atmosphere complemented with custom paneling of rich, red oak solids and veneers with a distressed finish. (floor plans, right)

(opposite) A premier hospitality venue of the Opryland Hotel and Convention Center in Nashville is Beauregard's, where classic black and white marble flooring, fluted columns, and leaded glass intimate a nineteenth Century plantation mansion.

PHOTOS: JONATHAN HILLYER

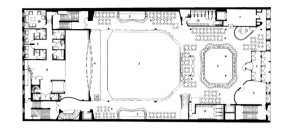

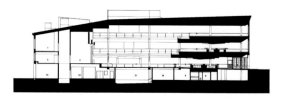

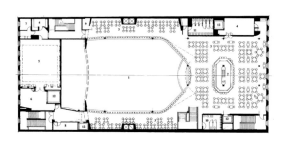

(above, left) Two abandoned warehouses on a historic Nashville Street were transformed into the Wildhorse Saloon, a three-level restaurant/dance hall and television production facility. Wrapping around the Wildhorse central bar, with a focus leading toward the dance floor, is a signature paisley bandanna pattern created by an innovative water jet process.

(left) From the technician's mezzanine at Wildhorse, papier-mâché wild horses define the venue's theme as they are seen crashing through the wall, while others gallop upside-down across the ceiling.
PHOTOS: NORMAN MCGRATH

(above) One of the two oak sidebars in Wildhorse undulates as fiber optics bounce across the soffit. A pink neon ridge line adds "electricity."

MATHIAS THÖRNER DESIGN, INC.

Mathias Thörner gravitates to a modern sensibility, softened by interesting and unusual uses of common materials. For instance, the sparkle of thousands of shiny shoe eyelets embedded in the concrete floor at Timberland's Chicago store reflect the unique personality of the client. Mathias Thörner started his interior design firm in Munich over twenty years ago and, ten years later, set his sights on Manhattan. Thörner still operates both offices, commuting between and often involving both offices on larger projects, now made possible by technology. With the initial aim to assist European clients expanding to America, and conversely, American companies expanding in Europe, he has developed a niche in retail, showroom, and office design for international fashion companies It is equally comfortable working within an existing shop system or designing entirely new ones

(right, top) A new double-height Timberland is housed in the former lobby of an Art Deco building in Chicago. The store is very contemorary yet, because of its simplicity, it does not distract from the more decorative vocabulary of the structure. The nautically inspired staircase links Timberland's first and second floors. Low, curved oak walls display footwear.

(right, bottom) "Outdoor" materials—granite, slate and concrete—are used to convey the rugged image of Timberland's merchandise.

(opposite) Building restrictions prohibited the use of a true second floor in this portion of the space. The solution was a metal catwalk along the perimeter from which merchandise can be displayed and customers can view the first floor from above.

ALL PHOTOS: ANDREW BORDWIN

(top) The existing structure of a former stable was retained and designated to house sports collection of Britches of Georgetown in Washington, D.C. Other merchandise groups are arranged around this core area.

(above) The entrance to Britches complies with the historical district's code restrictions. A contemporary, sporty image is projected through a classical glass and metal storefront. Signage was kept understated to not distract from the simplicity of the design.

(right) Open wooden frames amid an otherwise industrial-looking display system accentuate Britches' advertising photos and featured merchandise groups.

The M Street Collection

Feel the revitalization of an era. A time when dressing
was an art form. The M Street collection is inspired from
classic clothing for those who believe in personal style.

II BY IV DESIGN ASSOCIATES

Headquartered in Toronto, Canada, II BY IV Design Associates is an award-winning firm of interior designers whose work for hospitality, retail, and corporate clients is internationally recognized. Principals Dan Menchions and Keith Rushbrook have proven themselves as valuable members of their clients' marketing teams, creating environments that are highly functional as well as highly imaginative. Their approach is "thinking magically, designing practically." Canadian and American interior design associations and publications have honored II BY IV with more than forty awards of excellence for their innovative designs for restaurants, nightclubs, exhibits, showrooms, offices, furniture, and furnishings. The firm is especially well-known for its attention to lighting as a key interior design element, and has also received awards from the Illuminating Engineering Society of North America.

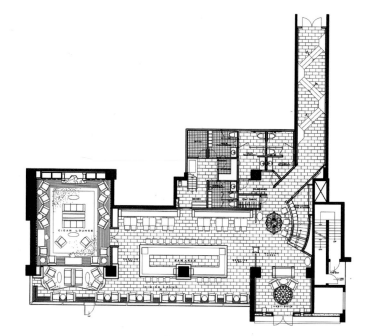

(right) Soft light cast on gold leaf ceiling patterns, brick, limestone, cedar, figured anigre, and yellow granite create the golden ambiance that gives the restaurant its name: Oro.

(opposite, top) Renovation of the Toronto restaurant Oro included reusing 1920s furniture pieces, elegant alabaster light fixtures, and several stained glass windows.

(opposite, bottom) The waiting area of Moishes, a 10,000-square-foot (900-square-meter) steak house in Toronto, uses wood, brick, and stone finishes and sensuous shapes to introduce a graceful yet bold image. (floor plan, right)

ALL PHOTOS: DAVID WHITTAKER

(left) Floating ribbons of drywall outlined in light break up Moishes' vast dining room ceiling. They also reduce sound reflection, as do the high-backed chairs that create intimate seating groups.

(below) Reflecting the simple, body-conscious character of Marccain, a European clothing line, the minimalist design features creamy polished plaster walls and slate floor. In Toronto, Marccain's highly efficient merchandising system of backlit maple "floating" panels with simple metal grommets supports shelving, hang rods, and front face display units that also provide an elegant background for mannequins.

(right) A cavernous, former bank site has been transformed into Zoom, a playful, sophisticated restaurant and lounge in Toronto. Materials, finishes, furniture, and lighting create a graceful, human scale. (floor plan, below)

(below) A "screen" of suspended magnifying lenses "look" into Zoom's elegant dining room. The fanciful ironwork of the furniture is a balanced contrast to the tall windows treated with sandblasted film and sheer indigo fabric and metal drapery.

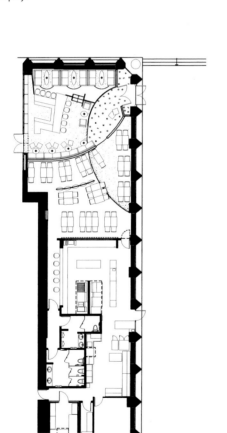

JEAN-PIERRE VIAU DESIGN

There are good reasons why Jean-Pierre Viau has become one of Montréal's most prolific designers. His guiding philosophy is evident in each project, where spaces are imbued with unexpected movement, and function defines form. He makes walls tilt and partitions curve, and provides unexpected openings onto other spaces. His textural contrasts surprise, his combinations of materials startle. While Viau does undertake private projects, his most visible achievements have been interiors for restaurants, shops, salons, showrooms, and offices. His highly original designs have led to exciting environments and great success for his clients. A graduate of Université du Québec à Montréal Environmental Design program, Viau worked until 1988 as an interior designer for a number of firms before founding his own. The following year, he burst onto the trendy Montréal scene with back-to-back openings of two establishments with vastly different callings—the fashion boutique F.O.O.D. and Citrus Restaurant.

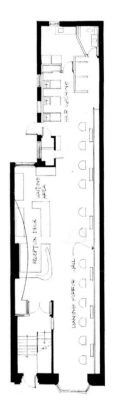

(above) Platine, a popular Montréal hair salon, uses maple veneer, chrome, and steel in clean lines inspired by 1950s minimalism. A splash of the dramatic is provided by a boomerang-shaped black shelf that swirls atop the angular reception desk at Platine. Styling stations sit in front of a canted mirror wall that runs the length of the deep, narrow space. Pale, striped vinyl floor tiles enhance the sense of depth. (floor plan, right)
PHOTO: MARC CRAMER

(opposite, top) One section of styling stations in Orbite Coupe Beauté in Montréal sits behind a sinuous wall of corrugated, translucent fiberglass, which offers clients privacy and still allows natural light from perimeter windows to filter into the reception/retail area.
PHOTO: AVENTURE STUDIO

(opposite, bottom) The Thaï Grill in Montréal uses warm wood, wicker, rattan, and a palette inspired by spices and open markets to evoke exotic travels without resorting to clichés. The bar features green slate flooring and wood shutters, adding a Colonial touch.
PHOTO: JEAN LONGPRE

(right) One of the leading Japanese restaurants in Montréal, Mikado has a Zen-like ambiance with contemporary rather than folkloric overtones. Broad, open planes are animated by a geometric motif inspired by the curvilinear shape of the *Katana* saber. Large curves incised into the wall and thrown into relief by lights that slide along the walls create a spare yet embracing atmosphere.

(below) Mikado's tatami room offers the intimacy to dine in traditional Japanese style behind elegant sliding screens made of rice paper and metal. The sweeping steel sculpture is one of two by Viau commissioned by the owner.

(opposite) Montréal's popular Pizzédélic restaurant presents a spare but warm and playful ambiance for a young, hip clientele. A focal point—a lowered ceiling made of translucent blue fiberglass set in metallic rings—reinforces the convivial ambiance.

PHOTOS: MARC CRAMER

YABU PUSHELBERG

Yabu Pushelberg is a Canadian-based international design practice established in 1980. With a staff of thirty-five design, technical, and management professionals, the firm undertakes corporate, retail, and hospitality projects throughout North America, Europe, and the Pacific Rim. A comprehensive range of services includes graphic design, marketing strategies, and visual merchandising concepts. Many clients are among the world's leading retailers, such as Escada, Club Monaco, Holt Renfrew, and Capezio. In addition, the firm has created lines of furnishings and carpets as an outgrowth of custom designs frequently incorporated into projects. These are manufactured and marketed under licensing agreements with ICF/Nienkämper, Louis Furniture, and Elte Carpets.

(right) The Men's Fragrances area at Holt Renfrew includes a traditional, masculine basin with streamlined wall-mounted fixtures. The display is accessible and familiar, encouraging customers to explore and test products.

(opposite) From the Information Zone at the front of ClearNet's flagship store in Toronto, Canada, clients can see clearly defined areas. Product information and floor models are accessed from pole fixtures offering self-guided information without commitment or intimidation.

PHOTOS: ROBERT BURLEY, DESIGN ARCHIVE

(below) At ClearNet's mineral water bar, clients wait for service applications to be processed. This amenity plays off the company's emphasis on "clear" communication. An adjacent area offers access to the ClearNet Website and brochures.

(right) Conversation niches are defined by translucent screens incorporating ClearNet graphics. They provide privacy for clients signing up for cell phone service. Table and sideboard fixtures add a residential atmosphere, aided by oversized "lampshade" fixtures overhead.

PHOTOS: ROBERT BURLEY, DESIGN ARCHIVE

(left, top) At the Holt Renfrew flagship store in Toronto, a custom hang-rod system allows the Left Bank department to make ample use of "story-boarding" merchandise combinations. Polished aluminum screens attract attention and contribute to the department's 1970s-inspired sensibility.
PHOTO: ROBERT BURLEY, DESIGN ARCHIVE

(left, bottom) In Toronto's Monsoon restaurant, the translucent acrylic wall between the men's and women's washrooms evokes the Oriental concept of shaping interior space with movable partitions, while providing a provocative hint of nightclub voyeurism.
PHOTO: EVAN DION

(right) Holt Renfrew's Men's Suits and Furnishings departments employ robin's egg blue, warm white, and dark wood to convey "tradition modernized." The fixtures update the haberdasher's traditional glass-fronted cabinets, and the custom seating is a streamlined version of the classic club chair.

(below) The Holt Renfrew Women's Collection is showcased using simple yet theatrical fixturing, featuring the HR Collection's signature colors—red for "runway" and black for "proscenium."
PHOTOS: ROBERT BURLEY, DESIGN ARCHIVE

ROBERT YOUNG ASSOCIATES

With more than thirty-three years devoted exclusively to retail design, Robert Young Associates (RYA) has created over 35 million square feet of retail space, ranging from major department stores to one-of-a-kind boutiques. RYA focuses on creating design solutions that are an integral part of a client's overall strategic plans. Services include project definition and scope, image positioning, interior, lighting, and graphic design, and all construction-related project management. The award-winning firm has served many of the finest chain and specialty retailers in the U.S. and overseas, including Bloomingdale's, Tiffany & Co., Neiman Marcus, Bon Marché, JCPenney, and Sulka.

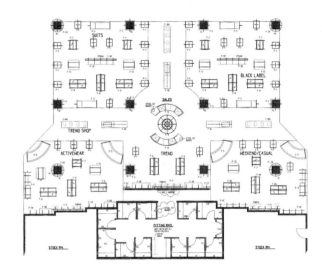

(above) At the I.N.C. prototype shop in Macy's Herald Square, New York, the crescent-shaped cashwrap, anchored by a circular "icon" fixture for graphic presentations, also offers customers seating for wardrobe consultations. The white flooring is softened with islands of green stone and sisal-like carpet. (floor plan, right)
PHOTO: ELLIOT KAUFMAN

(opposite) The Old World authenticity of the Beretta Gallery in Dallas, Texas, is inspired by the gun manufacturer's 471-year history. Wall cases of Cordovan-stained mahogany form clusters of "shops" with onyx and nickel pendant chandeliers and custom-designed furnishings.
PHOTO: IRA MONTGOMERY

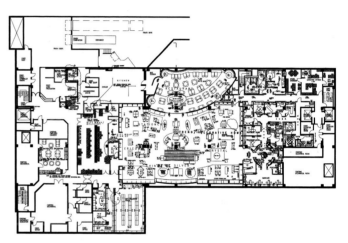

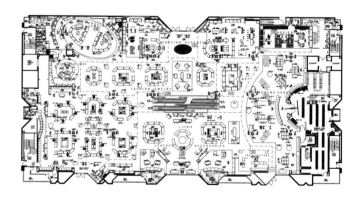

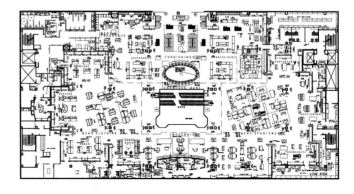

(top) Neiman Marcus windows overlooking Beverly Hills set the tone for Men's World using two 13-foot-long (3.9-meter-long) paintings by Dallas artist Michael Smith. An elliptical bar offers fine spirits and video monitors for those who either shopped 'til they dropped or are gathering a second wind. (floor plans, right)

(above) The designer shoe collection is anchored by a curved, backlit translucent screen behind display shelves. The sculpted space is defined by an illuminated curved dropped ceiling, a bright blue waxed plaster wall, and classic, residential seating and tables.

PHOTOS: PAUL BIELENBERG

(right) The renovation of Neiman Marcus-North Park, in Dallas, Texas, includes the Precious Jewels Salon. A dramatic yet unobtrusive backdrop for the spectacular merchandise is created by a light-washed barrel vault ceiling, mahogany paneling with incised satin nickel trim, satin stainless steel wall cases with black lacquer trim and handmade bronze medallions, and panels of biscuit-colored waxed Venetian stucco.

(below) Hand-carved, gold-leafed wood panels crown the individual wall cases lining the couture salon at Neiman Marcus-North Park. Recessed, gold-leafed vitrines showcase accessories, and a domed skylight brings natural light into the space.

PHOTOS: IRA MONTGOMERY

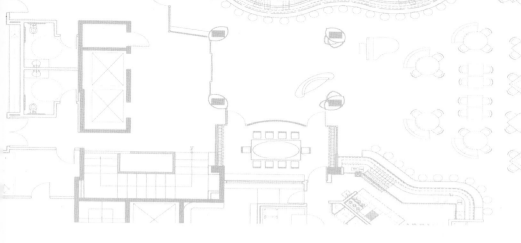

DIRECTORY OF FIRMS

AkarStudio
1404 Third Street Promenade
Suite 201
Santa Monica, California 90401
310-393-0625
Fax: 310-395-7692

Architectural Alliance Inc.
400 Clifton Avenue South
Minneapolis, Minnesota 55403-3299
612-871-5703
Fax: 612-871-7212

Aria Group Architects, Inc.
1100 Lake Street
Oak Park, Illinois 60301
708-445-8400
Fax: 708-445-1788

Axis Network Design Consultants
Sdn Bhd
Wisma Central
Jalan Ampang
50450 Kuala Lumpur, Malaysia
603-263-4181
FAX: 603-263-4186

Bergmeyer Associates, Inc.
286 Congress Street
Boston, Massachusetts 02210
617-542-1025
Fax: 617-338-6897

Bogdanow Partners Architects
75 Spring Street
New York, New York 10012
212-966-0313
Fax: 212-941-8875

Brennan Beer Gorman Monk/Interiors
515 Madison Avenue
New York, New York 10022
212-888-7663
Fax: 212-935-3868

Clodagh Design International
670 Broadway
New York, New York 10012
212-780-5300
Fax: 212-780-5755

CREAR - Jaime Bouzaglo
4860 Plamondon, #12
Montréal, Québec H3W 1E6
Canada
514-488-0594
Fax: 514-483-1379

Cuningham Group
201 Main Street, SE
Minneapolis, Minnesota 55414
612-379-3400
Fax: 612-379-4400

Desgrippes Gobé & Associates
411 Lafayette Street
New York, New York 10003
212-979-8900
Fax: 212-979-1401

Elkus/Manfredi Architects Ltd.
530 Atlantic Avenue
Boston, Massachusetts 02210
617-426-1300
Fax: 617-426-7502

Engstrom Design Group
1414 Fourth Street
San Rafael, California 94901
415-454-2277
Fax: 415-454-2278

FRCH Design Worldwide
311 Elm Street
Cincinnati, Ohio 45202
513-241-3000
Fax: 513-241-5015

Franke, Gottsegen, Cox Architects
443 Greenwich Street
New York, New York 10013
212-334-1191
Fax: 212-334-1317

Gensler
600 California Street
San Francisco, California 94108
415-433-3700
Fax: 415-627-3739

GRID/3 International
37 West 39 Street
New York, New York 10018
212-391-1162
Fax: 212-575-2391

Haverson Architecture and Design, P.C.
289 Greenwich Avenue
Greenwich, Connecticut 06830
203-629-8300
Fax: 203-629-8399

Hirsch Bedner Associates
3216 Nebraska Avenue
Santa Monica, California 90404
310-829-9087
Fax: 310-453-1182

IIDA Singapore PTE LTD
Space Planning & Interior Architecture
196C Geyland Road, Ying Lie Building
Singapore 389261
(65) 745-5288
Fax: (65) 747-2227

International Design Group, Inc.
188 Avenue Road
Toronto, Ontario M5R 2J1
Canada
416-961-1811
Fax: 416-961-9734

JGA, Inc.
29355 Northwestern Highway
Suite 300
Southfield, Michigan 48034
248-355-0890
Fax: 248-355-0895

Planungsgruppe Jöhnk
Wandsbeker Königstrasse 50
D-22041 Hamburg
Germany
(49) (0) 40-689421-0
Fax: (40) (0) 40-689221-30

SFJones-Architects
4218 Glencoe Avenue
Studio Two
Marina Del Rey, California 90292
310-822-3822
Fax: 310-306-4441

Lemay Michaud Architecture Design
740 William
Montréal, Quebec H3C 1P1
Canada
514-397-8737
Fax: 514-397-8739

Lieber Cooper Associates
444 North Michigan Avenue
Suite 1200
Chicago, Illinois 60611
312-527-0800
Fax: 312-527-3159

David Ling Architects
110 East 17th Street
New York, New York 10003
212-982-7089
Fax: 212-475-1336

John Lum Architecture
3246 17th Street
San Francisco, California 94110
415-753-0339
Fax: 415-753-2233

Michael Malone Architects, Inc.
13355 Noel Road, LB 58, Suite 1310
Dallas, Texas 75240
972-702-7960
Fax: 972-702-7975

Patrick McBride Company
2665 South Bayshore Drive, Suite 700
Coconut Grove, Florida 33133
305-858-7447
Fax: 305-858-9852

Jordan Mozer & Associates
320 W. Ohio Street
Chicago, Illinois 60610
312-397-1133
Fax: 312-397-1233

NBBJ
111 South Jackson
Seattle, Washington 98104
206-223-5134
Fax: 206-621-2305

Rita St. Clair Associates
1009 N. Charles Street
Baltimore, Maryland 21201
410-752-1313
Fax: 410-752-1335

Rockwell Group
Architecture, Planning and Design
5 Union Square West
New York, New York 10003
212-463-0334
Fax: 212-463-0335

Shea Architects, Inc.
Butler Square, Suite 650C
100 N. Sixth Street
Minneapolis, Minnesota 55403
612-339-2257
Fax: 612-349-2930

Earl Swensson Associates, Inc.
2100 West End Avenue, Suite 1200
Nashville, Tennessee 37203
615-329-9445
Fax: 615-329-0046

Mathias Thörner Design, Inc.
40 West 22nd Street
New York, New York 10010
212-675-1170
Fax: 212-675-9061

II BY IV Design Associates
77 Mowat Avenue
Toronto, Ontario M6J 3E3
Canada
416-531-2224
Fax: 416-531-4460

Jean-Pierre Viau Design
55 Mont-Royal Avenue West #801
Montréal, Québec H2T 2S6
Canada
514-844-4383
Fax: 514-282-9151

Yabu Pushelberg
55 Booth Avenue
Toronto, Ontario M4M 2M3
Canada
416-778-9779
Fax: 416-778-9747

Robert Young Associates
3100 McKinnon Street
Dallas, Texas 75201
214-220-9050
Fax: 214-220-9047

DIRECTORY OF RETAIL AND RESTAURANT PROJECTS

RETAIL

AKRIS,
Boston, Massachusetts 28

Ann Taylor, Madison Avenue,
New York, New York 50

The Artful Hand,
Boston, Massachusetts 54

Audi Park Avenue,
New York, New York 82

Aveda,
New York, New York 74

Bailey, Banks & Biddle,
Philadelphia, Pennsylvania 100

Baretta Gallery,
Dallas, Texas 184

Best Cellars,
New York, New York 150

Blue Canoe,
Seattle, Washington 134

Boston Museum of Fine Arts
Museum Store,
Boston, Massachusetts 24

Bottle Your Own,
Toronto, Canada 100

Britches,
Georgetown, Washington, D.C. 168

Brookstone,
New York, New York 104

Camelot Music,
Great Lakes Mall, Ohio 104

Carnival Corner, Harrah's,
Las Vegas, Nevada 66

Christian Bernard, Roosevelt
Field Mall,
Long Island, New York 84

ClearNet,
Toronto, Canada 178, 180

Comp USA, Fifth Avenue,
New York, New York 34

Compaq Works,
Houston, Texas 79

Color Siete,
Bogotá, Columbia 85

Coppola Boutique,
Montréal, Canada 42

Dick's Clothing and Sporting Goods,
Columbia, Maryland 26

Discovery Channel Store,
The Galleria,
Houston, Texas 134

Dr. Jimmy Fong Optometry,
San Francisco, California 130

Eddie Bauer, Michigan Avenue
Chicago, Illinois 70

Eddie Bauer,
San Francisco, California 70

Elizabeth Arden Red Door,
Madison Avenue,
New York, New York 106

Famous Players Silver City,
Toronto, Canada 98

FEC II Center,
Stüttgart, Germany 111

Felissimo,
New York, New York 38, 40

Foot Locker,
Watertown, Massachusetts 58

Fossil,
Columbus, Ohio 106

Giorgio Beverly Hills,
Beverly Hills, California 106

Haute Coiffure Salon, Starhill Centre,
Kuala Lumpur, Malaysia 22

Holt Renfrew,
Toronto, Canada 178, 182, 183

HomeChef,
Palo Alto, California 80

I.N.C., Macy's Herald Square,
New York, New York 184

Jackpot, Harrah's,
Las Vegas, Nevada 68

Kids Foot Locker,
Watertown, Massachusetts 58

La Maison du Cigar,
Beverly Hills, California 112

La Maison Simons Department Store,
Québec City, Canada 100

Levi Strauss Dockers Store,
Troy, Michigan 28

Liz Claiborne,
New York, New York 52

Marccain,
Toronto, Canada 172

Mr. Rags,
Bellevue, Washington 144, 147

Neiman Marcus,
Beverly Hills, California 186

Neiman Marcus-North Park,
Dallas, Texas 186, 187

Nöelle Spa for Beauty & Wellness,
Stamford, Connecticut 38

The North Face,
Chicago, Illinois 78

Orbite Coupe Beauté,
Montréal, Canada 174

OshKosh B'Gosh,
Leawood, Kansas 68

Philosophy Boutique for
Alberta Ferretti,
New York, New York 124, 126

Platine,
Montréal, Canada 174

Puget Consumers Co-op,
Seattle, Washington 147

Rockport Company,
New York, New York 53

Runner's Choice,
Toronto, Canada 98

San Francisco Museum of
Modern Art Museum Store,
San Francisco, California 80

Shell Oil's Encompass Store,
Houston, Texas 132

SOMA Living,
San Francisco, California 80

Star Trek: The Experience,
Las Vegas, Nevada 46

Stüttgart Candy Shop,
Stüttgart, Germany 111

Tempus Expeditions,
Mall of America,
Bloomington, Minnesota 66

Timberland,
Chicago, Illinois 166

Transporter: Movies You Ride,
Empire State Building,
New York, New York 34

Turnbull & Asser,
New York, New York 88

Universal Studios Store,
Hollywood, California 76

Urban Eyes Optometry,
San Francisco, California 131

Voyagers: The Travel Store,
Plano, Texas 132

Warner Bros., Fifth Avenue,
New York, New York 102

World of Disney Store,
Downtown Disney,
Orlando, Florida 56

RESTAURANTS

American Bistro,
Thousand Oaks, California 10

Apollo Bar,
Cologne, Germany 126

Asia SF,
San Francisco, California 130

Baang,
Aspen, Colorado 152

Bar Biloxi,
Montréal, Canada 118

Barney Greengrass,
Barney's New York,
Beverly Hills, California 72

Beauregard's, Opryland Hotel and
Convention Center,
Nashville, Tennessee 162

Bice Ristorante,
Montréal, Canada 42

Big Downtown, Palmer House,
Chicago, Illinois 120

Bistango,
Québec City, Canada 116, 119

Bistro Blechnapf,
Neümunster, Germany 108

Brio, Blue Chip Casino,
Michigan City, Indiana 16

Café Blue Veranda, Hotel Inter-
Continental,
Tokyo Bay, Tokyo 90

Café Carnaval,
Westin Rio Mar Resort,
Puerto Rico 90

Café du Monde,
Québec, Canada 119

Café Odyssey, Mall of America,
Bloomington, Minnesota 48

Café Site,
Seoul, Korea 104

Café Spiaggia,
Chicago, Illinois 120

California Café,
Denver, Colorado 60, 62

California Café Bar and Grill,
Chicago, Illinois 62

Caribou Coffee,
Brooklyn Park, Minnesota 12

Caribou Coffee,
Woodbury, Minnesota 14

Charleston Restaurant,
Baltimore, Maryland 154, 156

Cheesecake Factory,
Chicago, Illinois 142

Cilantro, Micasa Hotel,
Kuala Lumpur, Malaysia 20, 22

Coco Marina,
New York, New York 136

Commonwealth Brewing Company,
Rockefeller Center,
New York, New York 24

Coral and Shell Club,
Boat Quay, Singapore 96

The Cup,
University of Minnesota 158

Cypress Club,
Chicago, Illinois 142

David Paul's Diamond Head Grill,
Colony Surf Hotel,
Honolulu, Hawaii 114

Diva Discotheque,
Montréal, Canada 42

Famous Dave's,
Forest Lake, Minnesota 161

FEC II Brewery,
Stüttgart, Germany 111

56 West,
Chicago, Illinois 18

Fulton's Crab House, Pleasure Island,
Walt Disney World Resort,
Orlando, Florida 122

Goodfellow's,
Minneapolis, Minnesota 158, 160

Hard Rock Café,
Key West, Florida 138

Harley-Davidson Café,
Las Vegas, Nevada 89

Heaven on Seven,
Chicago, Illinois 18

Ho Wan, Sheraton Desert Inn,
Las Vegas, Nevada 93

The Hump, Santa Monica Airport,
Santa Monica, California 115

Hyatt Regency Aruba, Dining Room,
Aruba 90

Jimmy Buffet's Margaritaville,
Charleston, South Carolina 138

Kublai Khan Restaurant,
Park Mall Shopping Centre,
Singapore 94

La Cucina, Hotel Europa & Regina,
Venice, Italy 92

Mediterraneo,
Montréal, Canada 44

Merchants,
New York, New York 32

Mi Piace,
Los Angeles, California 8

App Mikado,
Montréal, Canada 176

Moishes,
Toronto, Canada 170, 172

Monkey Bar,
New York, New York 152

Monsoon,
Toronto, Canada 182

Motown Café,
New York Hotel and Casino,
Las Vegas, Nevada 86

Next Door Nobu,
New York, New York 148

Ninth Street Pub,
Taiwan 96

Nobu,
New York, New York 150

Nordsee,
Frankfurt, Germany 108

Nordstrom Café,
Atlanta, Georgia 64

O'Padeiro,
New York, New York 75

Oro,
Toronto, Canada 170

Palmer House Hilton, Main Dining Room,
Chicago, Illinois 122

PapaRazzi's Cucina Ristorante,
Peabody, Massachusetts 54

Paradis,
Palo Alto, California 128

Payard Patisserie and Bistro,
New York, New York 152

Peabody Court
Restaurant/Conservatory,
Baltimore, Maryland 156

Peninsula Hong Kong
Hotel Restaurant,
Hong Kong 36

Pizzédélic,
Montréal, Canada 176

Pointe des Amerique,
Montréal, Canada 118

Polo Grill,
Baltimore, Maryland 156

Portofino Restaurant,
Sheraton Desert Inn,
Las Vegas, Nevada 92

Prímadonna Restaurant,
Montréal, Canada 45

Rain,
New York, New York 32

Rainforest Café, Disney Marketplace,
Lake Buena Vista, Florida 48

Rockcafé,
Stüttgart, Germany 111

Slick Willie's Bayou Place,
Houston, Texas 79

Sola Squeeze,
Minneapolis, Minnesota 14

Spiga Ristorante,
New York, New York 86

Stir Crazy,
Northbrook, Illinois 122

Straits Restaurant, Radisson Plaza,
Kuala Lumpur, Malaysia 20

Stüttgart Candy Shop,
Stüttgart, Germany 111

Surf'n Turf,
Matsuyama, Japan 140, 142

Tejas,
Edina, Minnesota, ...160

Thai Grill,
Montréal, Canada 174

Trilogy Café, Bangsar,
Kuala Lumpur, Malaysia 20

Tuscan Square, Rockefeller Center,
New York, New York 136

Union Pacific Restaurant,
New York, New York 30

Ventura Lounge, Blue Chip Casino,
Michigan City, Indiana 16

The Verandah, Peninsula Hong Kong
Hotel ,Hong Kong 36

Vertigo, TransAmerica Tower,
San Francisco, California 65

Wildhorse Saloon,
Nashville, Tennessee 164

Zoom,
Toronto, Canada 173